Thank You!

I0521593

Thank you for your purchase.

I am dedicated to making the most enriching and informational content. I hope it meets your expectations and you gain a lot from it.

Your comments and feedback are important to me because they help me to provide the best material possible. So, if you have any questions or concerns, please email me at richardbanks.books@gmail.com.

Again, thank you for your purchase.

STRESS AND YOUR HEALTH

The Most Effective Guide on How to Deal with Stress, Lower Cortisol Levels, Avoid Burnout, and Live a Life Filled with Happiness and Well-Being

Richard Banks

INTRODUCTION

We often say, "this is stressful!" or "I'm so stressed out!" But what is stress, really? Stress is a mental, physical, or behavioral reaction to any perceived demand or threat. Our minds and bodies continuously put demands on each other, and if we feel we do not possess the ability to cope with these demands, we feel stressed.

We all are likely to feel stressed when we perceive a situation as dangerous, complex, or painful. Stress also occurs when we believe that we don't have the resources to cope with a situation. From the pandemic to economic pressures, political tensions, and natural

9

disasters, the start of the new decade has seemed to throw one stressor after another. It's no wonder everyone seems stressed these days. We become troubled and anxious if our demands are more than we can manage.

Stress has been dubbed the "Health Epidemic of the 21st Century" by the World Health Organization and is estimated to cost American businesses up to $300 billion annually. The effect of stress on our emotional and physical health can be devastating. Between 1983 and 2009, stress levels increased by 10–30% among all demographic groups in the USA.

The body will signal that we are overstressed through physical symptoms, such as muscle tension, sweaty palms, headaches or migraines, gastrointestinal issues, clenched or grinding teeth, or difficulty sleeping. We might feel worry, fear, fatigue, irritability, or have difficulty concentrating. We might even isolate ourselves from others due to feelings of low self-esteem or overwhelm and agitation. These can be the signs of stress, but the consequences of too much stress can be severe for us and those around us.

Over 70% of all illnesses are either caused or worsened by stress. Over time, too much stress can increase heart rate, breathing rate, blood pressure, blood sugar, and muscle tension. It increases the risk of chronic disorders, including depression, anxiety, addiction, and obesity. It can also compromise the immune system. Long-term stress can eventually lead to cancer, Alzheimer's, and heart diseases.

The mind and body are integrated—they affect each other. Stress and stress response both begin in the nervous system. The nervous system releases the stress hormones cortisol and epinephrine throughout the body to prepare us for the *fight-or-flight* response. This response includes:

- Increased blood flow, heart rate, and blood pressure to provide extra energy
- Heightened senses to detect danger
- The release of stored energy—fats and sugars— to give the body an additional boost of power

The solution is to keep our stressors under control with stress management skills. These may include (among others) visualization skills, physical activities, talk therapies, and relaxation techniques to reduce our stress levels. Learning to master our negative thoughts will help us overcome stressful situations.

Because stress is anything that stimulates you or increases your level of alertness, we might think that any stress is bad. Yet, some stress can be considered positive as it acts as a motivator that helps you compete and excel towards bigger goals, which can add anticipation and excitement to life. Some people thrive on deadlines and competition. The anticipation of happy future events such as job promotions or the arrival of a new baby can also cause positive stress. Distress is the more familiar form of stress. However, eustress results from a "positive" view of an event or situation, which is why it is also called "good stress." Eustress helps you rise to a challenge and can be an antidote to boredom because it engages focused energy.

It is essential to notice situations that may potentially trigger our stress response. We can manage our stress by observing when we feel anxious, taking time to relax, balancing our diet, including using vitamins and supplements, finding solutions to long-term problems, and engaging in talk therapies.

Stress can be prevented or reduced considerably by planning and mentally preparing for moments we know may cause stress. Finding positive and healthy ways to control the harmful effects of stress on our minds and body can significantly increase our quality of life.

When we are faced with a stressful situation, it is a good idea to consider the four A's of stress management:

Avoid the Situation

Avoiding stress involves learning to say no—avoiding negative people, media, or situations that can elevate our stress levels.

Alter the Situation

Altering your stressor requires being willing to compromise to make stressors more manageable. Compromising on details or a deadline is often necessary. Time management is a crucial component of altering stress.

Accept the Situation

Many stressors that we face are inevitable. We may have no choice but to accept them. We should not try to control the uncontrollable, but focus on the only thing we can manage—our reaction. Accepting the stressor becomes possible when we look for the upside in challenging situations. Remember, challenges often lead to personal growth and prosperity.

Adapt to the Situation

Adapting to stressors includes looking at the bigger picture. Is what is bothering us today going to be a big deal in a month or a year? We can adjust our standards to be more reasonable.

Often, people have incorrect perceptions about stress. You might think that something should not stress you out because it doesn't cause stress for those around you. But everyone has unique emotional states and coping abilities.

One method of stress management is to be aware of our individual sources of stress. For example—if you are afraid of dogs, you may want to practice visualization or breathing techniques before visiting a friend with a corgi, even though others find the dog harmless. When we know our triggers, we can be more prepared to deal with them and practice skills to lower our stress levels.

There are many sources of stress. These include interpersonal (ending a relationship, for example), intrapersonal (worries about your job), and physiological stressors (being chased by a bear or a vicious corgi). Stress can't be avoided, but we can manage both our response to stressful situations and the long-term effects of stress on our bodies.

Getting trapped in the vicious cycle of stress can be physically and mentally exhausting. It reduces our productivity and lowers our quality of life. Crucially, many stress responses are unnecessary, and if we know how to deal with the triggering situations, we can reduce the threat to our wellbeing.

Unknown to us, our bodies retain stress—allowing it to grow and compound slowly, unnoticed and untreated, sometimes for years. If you've ever seen someone snap under pressure, you may have witnessed the culmination of years of untreated stress. Many people lack the motivation, guidance, or knowledge to address their stressors before reaching that breaking point. When you take control of your stressors and stress response, you take back the ability to be resourceful and mindful in all you do.

Everyone can benefit from mastering stress management skills. Making changes, even small ones, can reduce the burden of stress. Managing stress and committing ourselves to happiness are the keys to contented living. When stress management is done right, it opens the gates of joy and prosperity for ourselves and those around us.

This book will present you with healthy techniques and suggestions to help you reduce stress. You will learn about living in the moment, letting go of things that are out of your control, the benefits of practicing exercise and gratitude, and many other strategies to decrease stress and increase happiness. In these pages, you will
16

learn how to decide which situations require your time and attention, how to maintain a healthy balance between the competing demands in your life, and how to transform a stressful thought into productive activity.

CHAPTER 1: STRESS AND THE NERVOUS SYSTEM

"Stress is simply the adaptation of our bodies and minds to change." – **Peter G. Hanson, M.D.**

The Brain's Response to Stress

When someone experiences a stressful event, the amygdala—an area of the brain that contributes to emotional processing—sends a distress signal to the hypothalamus. This area of the brain communicates with the rest of the body so that the person has the energy to fight or flee.

The hypothalamus is a bit like a command center. It communicates with the rest of the body through the autonomic nervous system, which controls involuntary body functions such as breathing, blood pressure, heartbeat, and the dilation or constriction of key blood vessels.

After the amygdala sends a distress signal, the hypothalamus activates the sympathetic nervous system (SNS) by sending signals through the autonomic nerves to the adrenal glands. These glands respond by pumping the hormone epinephrine (also known as adrenaline) into the bloodstream. As epinephrine circulates through the body, it brings on several physiological changes. The heart beats faster than usual, pushing blood to the muscles, heart, and other vital organs. Pulse and blood pressure go up. The person undergoing these changes also starts to breathe more rapidly. Small airways in the lungs open wide. Extra oxygen is sent to the brain, increasing alertness. Blood clotting mechanisms are activated to control bleeding. Stored energy fuels show as sugar and fats are released to supply energy to all body parts. Sight, hearing, and other senses become sharper.

These changes happen so quickly that most people aren't aware of them. That's why someone could jump out of the path of an oncoming car even before thinking about what they are doing, for example.

The Autonomic Nervous System

The nervous system has several divisions—the central division involving the brain and spinal cord and the peripheral division consisting of the autonomic and somatic nervous systems. The autonomic nervous system supplies the internal processes of the human body, including the blood vessels, stomach, intestine, liver, kidneys, bladder, genitals, lungs, pupils, heart, and sweat, salivary, and digestive glands, which makes it an essential part of how people deal with stress.

The autonomic nervous system plays a direct role in the physical response to stress and is divided into the sympathetic nervous system (SNS) and the parasympathetic nervous system (PNS). When the

21

body is stressed, the SNS contributes to what is known as the *fight-or-flight* response. The body shifts its energy resources toward fighting off a life threat or fleeing from an enemy.

The autonomic nervous system is activated when the brain senses stress. It regulates visceral activities and vital organs. The autonomic nervous system's nerve connections communicate focus to the enteric (intestinal) nervous system.

Besides causing butterflies in your stomach, this brain-gut connection can disturb the natural rhythmic contraction that moves through your gut, leading to irritable bowel syndrome and increasing gut sensitivity to acid, making you more likely to feel heartburn. Not only this, but the visceral activities that the autonomic nervous system controls could also affect your metabolism and weight, your electrolytes and balance of water, and even your production and elimination of urine. Stress and the brain-body connection can truly throw your entire system out of whack.

Sympathetic Nervous System

The sympathetic nervous system is responsible for the responses associated with the fight-or-flight response. And this response or physical arousal is stimulated by releasing two hormones, epinephrine (adrenaline) and norepinephrine (noradrenaline). It prepares and signals the body to act. It gives a strong signal to the body to fight the stressor. This nervous system allows for increased muscular strength in case of a fight and causes your palms to sweat, pupils to dilate, and hair to stand on end. The sympathetic nervous system also slows body processes that are less important in emergencies, such as digestion and urination.

Parasympathetic Nervous System

The parasympathetic nervous system maintains homeostasis by releasing the hormone acetylcholine (ACH), which is responsible for energy conservation and relaxation of the body, usually during regular activity or when conserving and restoring the boy after a flight-or-fight response. This branch of the autonomic nervous system instructs our body to rest and relax when needed and helps slow down the body after a high-energy state of an active fight-or-flight stress response.

The autonomic nervous system's role in managing our fight-or-flight mode is activated when we experience a stressful situation. The body cannot stay in an active sympathetic state for long.

Initially, during a stress response, when the body responds to a flight-or-fight situation, the body is brought back to its original state. The sympathetic system switches off when the stressor is not there anymore. The parasympathetic system takes charge after a certain period of time. This step is vital for the conservation of the body.

If the heart keeps pumping the blood at a higher rate for a long time, then the body will not be able to sustain itself healthily for long. The parasympathetic nervous system has to take charge after the threat response or at the time when the stressor is removed.

Role of HPA in Stress Response

When the function of epinephrine is complete, the hypothalamus activates the second component of the stress response system, known as the hypothalamus-pituitary-adrenal axis or HPA axis.

This network is comprised of the following:

1. The hypothalamus

2. The adrenal glands

3. The pituitary gland

The HPA axis manages and keeps the sympathetic nervous system under control through hormonal signals. Stress begins with the HPA axis, which comprises a series of interactions between the brain's endocrine glands and the kidneys that control our body's response to the stressor. The HPA axis is instantly activated when the brain detects a stressful situation. It then releases the stress hormone cortisol, which primes the body for instant action. Through this process, the human body remains on high alert in the presence of a stressor.

However, the cortisol level drops back to normal when the stress passes. The relaxed state is achieved by the invasion of the parasympathetic nervous system to dampen the stress response.

Symptoms of High Stress Levels

Experiencing stressors over a prolonged period can result in a long-term drain on the body. As the autonomic nervous system continues to trigger physical reactions, it causes wear and tear on the body. It's not so much what chronic stress does to the nervous system but what continuous activation of the nervous system does to other bodily systems that becomes problematic.

Since our fast-paced routine has made most of us a victim of high stress levels, our bodies have to bear the cost of our exhausting ways of living. In phases of chronic stress, we begin to feel unpleasant and dangerous effects such as:

- Mood swings
- Anxiety or depression
- Weight gain

- Increase or loss of appetite
- Disturbed sleep or difficulty sleeping that eventually leads to insomnia
- Increased blood pressure
- Unexplained headaches
- Heartburn
- Irritability
- Fatigue
- Aggression
- Irregular menstrual cycle in females
- Muscle tension
- Becoming tired too quickly
- Feeling less motivated
- Frequent negative thoughts
- Digestive and intestinal problems, including constipation, bloating, or diarrhea

Eustress—The Positive Stress That Keeps You Going

Stress is an unavoidable reality of life. Yet, not all stress is dangerous or harmful. Some stress we experience can be more detrimental to our well-being, whereas other types of stress can prove beneficial.

One type of beneficial stress is eustress, which leads to a positive response and enables a person to contribute to a better environment. Eustress is contrary in meaning and nature to distress. It can refer to any beneficial stress that can improve an individual's mental and physiological health.

Characteristics of Eustress

Eustress can be identified and implemented easily to initiate positive life changes. It tends to be short-term and often feels exciting for a person, providing an extra positive push or energy toward building relationships and achieving goals.

Regarding physical symptoms, eustress can resemble a stressful situation as one begins to feel nervous, often accompanied by a pounding heartbeat and racing thoughts. How we perceive these physical sensations is what makes the difference.

In a state of eustress, one can feel a sense of excitement or anticipation. However, you may feel persistently uncomfortable and overwhelmed under anxiety and pressure.

Eustress is mandatory for overall development and growth. This type of positive stress can create a sense of long-term optimism and minimize negative thinking patterns.

Eustress in Our Daily Life

When it occurs in any situation or phase of life, eustress positively impacts the individual's life. Eustress is typically associated with feelings of excitement and challenge rather than anxiety or fear. Where stress can leave a person feeling demotivated and low on self-esteem, eustress can create a positive response and energy, resulting in rewarding conclusions. Generally, eustress can push someone outside their comfort zone and challenge them to step out of the familiar and rise to the new experience. The energy that someone with eustress feels can sustain the motivation to pursue and continue a challenging task.

Following are some examples of eustress from which we can learn its positive impact on our life and well-being:

Major Life Transitions

Specific life changes can create positive stress for an individual, such as starting a new relationship, being involved in a new business or trade, the birth of a child or parenting children, etc.

This type of stress induces a sense of responsibility in a person. Therefore, it is considered positive and even essential to get moving in life.

Minor Changes or A Short-Term Events

Eustress is usually short-term. Therefore, events or situations that happen for a short duration or particular period can create eustress. A few examples are as follows:

- When Exposed to Something Scary/Thrilling

Eustress is created when a person watches a scary movie that gives goosebumps. A person might be screaming while watching the movie, and some may sweat or even try to hide their faces during intense fearful movie scenes. But as the film reaches its climax, the created stress of that time starts diminishing, and the individual regains their state of relaxation. The eustress in this situation creates excitement for an individual and curiosity to know what may happen next.

One benefit of having such exposure is that it helps individuals overcome many of their fears, such as darkness, fear of loneliness, etc. Therefore, stress cannot be considered harmful in these cases, as it helps a person learn certain traits that otherwise would not have been retained in the absence of eustress.

- Enjoying Leisure Hours

A fun roller coaster ride might give thrills as a person feels stress and excitement, but during or after the ride, they feel great for the enjoyment they experienced in that moment.

- When Exposed to New Experiences

Whenever we have a new experience, we feel a positive driving force or eustress. New experiences are often related to significant discomfort and increased fear of uncertainty for specific individuals. However, its positive impact on a person's well-being is far more long-lasting than the short initial doubt.

For instance, traveling to an unfamiliar place for the first time can make a person feel uncertain regarding the outcome of such travel. But it can later lead to new discoveries and increased knowledge of the new place's culture, norms, behaviors, business trends, etc.

Things done for the first time will create eustress and excitement for an individual, such as the anticipation of the first date with your lover, first day at your job, your first speech in public, and many other exciting firsts that fall under the umbrella of eustress.

The Impact of Eustress

Positive stress is necessary and needs to be present in our lives. A perfect life would never make a person learn or grow. Slight pressure at safe levels in the form of eustress should exist in people's lives, so they know their potential and set their objectives and boundaries.

The positive effects that eustress can bring include the following:

- Aid in concentration and focus
- Increase in motivation levels
- Encouragement to strive for future goals
- Help to identify the meaning and purpose of living
- Help to develop a better personality
- Resilience in times of challenges
- Creating long-term happiness
- Providing a significant contribution toward physical and mental health

Eustress in balance is essential for our growth and progress. It enhances performance and creates motivational self-talk that quickly helps us overcome many stressors.

An optimal approach to stress can increase our performance at work. Arousal in the form of positive stress is not harmful to us—it is encouraged and even considered vital to carry a certain amount of pressure to help us experience the realities of life to the fullest.

Without this push provided by eustress, we would not be motivated to strive for better things and achievements in life.

Eustress in the Workplace

An excellent example of eustress can be seen in an organizational setting. Different tasks can be accomplished through various levels of arousal and stress. For instance, Austin develops eustress for submitting the financial statements of a tobacco company for which he works as a finance manager.

The arousal and stress he feels during those few days are the positive driving force that boosts his mind and body, giving him extra energy to finish the work and meet the deadline quickly.

If he did not feel such stimulation or eustress, he would lag in submitting the financials and may make excuses to his employer by making up a false story. Without an inner motivation, we would never feel boosted to complete tasks or fulfill assigned responsibilities.

No matter how strict the organizational rules can be,

no matter how much your coworkers encourage you, or how much your boss may motivate you by arranging sessions regarding improving employee performance—if the motivation is not within you, no one will be able to help you progress and flourish.

In workplaces with constant competition between employees, pressure regarding promotions, stress about presentations, or strict rules regarding completion of goals, eustress helps in every aspect.

Working under pressure and meeting challenges make people more substantial in mind, thoughts, and willpower and frequently lessens the personality flaws of low confidence and poor communication skills.

However, there are times when it is difficult to distinguish between stress and eustress. Here are some warning signs to look for:

- Inability to concentrate or complete tasks
- Get sick more often with colds
- Body aches

- Other illnesses like autoimmune diseases flare up
- Headaches
- Irritability
- Trouble falling sleeping or staying awake
- Changes in appetite
- More angry or anxious than usual

From Distress to Eustress

It is crucial to note that there are events and situations where one's distress can be transformed into eustress.

For instance, distress could be caused by experiencing a breakup with the person you had thought to spend your entire life with or facing job loss, not because of your negligence but because your firm is facing irrecoverable loss.

Such changes can be initially upsetting. You may begin to question yourself and your qualities, such as your relationship intimacy or job abilities. This temporary imbalance due to life change can be perceived as an opportunity for change and growth over time.

You may become stronger than ever when you lose someone you love, and you can uncover many hidden qualities previously unknown to you after facing a setback in your workplace.

CHAPTER 2: WHAT WE THINK AFFECTS OUR BEHAVIOR

"The truth is that stress doesn't come from your boss, your kids, your spouse, traffic jams, health challenges, or other circumstances. It comes from your thoughts about your circumstances."
—Andrew Bernstein

Most people have a silent conversation with themselves for much of the day. This internal dialogue can direct our thoughts and behaviors. Understanding what self-talk is and how it affects you is the first step in learning how to rewrite your own self-talk "script" and talk your way to a less stressful way of life.

Our self-talk plays a significant role in keeping our minds intact and our personal and social life happy. If our self-talk is negative, it will lead to low self-esteem, which drastically affects our behavior patterns. The following traits appear as a consequence of negative thinking:

- Reluctance to meet new people, and loss of interest in a job or educational institute
- Avoidance of socializing with friends and family and preferring isolation over social gatherings
- Generally feeling nervous and avoiding volunteering for presentations, workshops, etc.
- Loss of friends due to a suspicious nature
- Circle of friends growing smaller, and many times being left alone due to persistent negative behavior
- Feeling unwelcomed by close associates
- Finding it hard to enjoy leisure time due to anxiety and depression

- Observable changes in a person's weight and eating habits, indulging in binge eating or becoming obese or very weak

Cognitive Distortions

Negative, irrational thinking patterns are called *cognitive distortions.* These negative thought patterns and emotions can interfere with a healthy routine by diminishing the drive to improve, lowering motivation levels, creating anxiety and depression, lowering self-esteem, and increasing the chances of substance use.

According to the American Psychological Association, anyone can experience a cognitive distortion. However, for most people, it is only a momentary difficulty, while for other's cognitive distortions have become a pattern of thinking that interfere with their daily lives and relationships. Distorted thinking can lead to chronic anxiety, depression, and behavioral problems such as substance abuse in these cases.

Cognitive distortions are thinking errors that can be

well managed by using professional techniques and approaches like cognitive behavioral therapy (CBT) to recognize these distortions and replace them with healthier, helpful, and positive thoughts.

There are different types of cognitive distortions. They all tend to induce some degree of anxiety and raise stress levels. Some examples of cognitive distortions are as follows:

Polarized Thinking

Also known as *all-or-nothing thinking* or *black-and-white thinking*, this type of thinking involves perceiving things in absolute terms. Individuals view the situation as either black or white, good or bad, success or failure, everything or nothing.

Limitations of Polarized Thinking

The major hurdle in this type of thinking is that it does not leave any room for an individual to think outside of extremes (good or bad).

It impairs an individual's confidence and motivation

and makes it harder to adhere to long-term goals. As a result, a person's chances of progress become low compared to those who do not possess such thinking.

Mental Disabilities Associated with Polarized Thinking

Black or white thinking may be associated with an underlying medical condition. These may include Borderline Personality Disorder (BPD) and Narcissistic Personality Disorder (NPD).

Real-life Examples

If you suffer from black-and-white thinking, you may be unable to maintain a healthy diet. This may happen because every time you try to stick to a healthy nutrition plan, you feel like giving up and calling yourself a failure each time you think of deviating from your diet plan.

You might feel like starting a new exercise plan to tone your body is not a good option for you. You feel hopeless and unmotivated even if you plan to start something. You may think starting a new workout plan is ineffective as you will not be able to give it 100%, and therefore you are a failure.

You might even feel like a failure in places where you have daily or frequent exposure, such as at school. As you learn, every time or situation you make a mistake, you might begin thinking you will not be able to do well. You will lack the ability to acknowledge the error and move past it.

Overgeneralization

This cognitive distortion occurs when you perceive something as permanent and final after experiencing a single coincidence or similar situation. The terms "always" or "never" are common to those suffering from overgeneralized thinking.

Limitations of Overgeneralization

Individuals may assume that all events will have the same outcome as the one situation they have experienced.

Another limitation of this cognitive distortion is that it does not consider the differences between situations and how chance or luck can affect events. Overgeneralization can have several consequences on thinking patterns and how people act in different situations.

Mental Disabilities Associated with Overgeneralization

Holding on to feelings of fear from one situation and overgeneralizing those feelings onto future events creates anxiety which may lead to mental disorders. Overgeneralization is associated with the development of certain mental and anxiety disorders.

When individuals experience one bad situation, they presume the same bad thing will happen again in future cases. This cognitive distortion is found in those with PTSD or post-traumatic stress disorder.

Real-life Example

One might presume from many coincidences that three is their lucky number and continue to use it in gambling situations, no matter how many times it results in failure and loss of fortune.

This would mean that the person is going through cognitive distortion in the form of overgeneralization.

Mental Filters

A mental filter refers to a distorted thought pattern in which an individual ignores positive experiences and ideas and believes exclusively in negative ones. Interpreting circumstances using negative mental filtering is unhealthy and leads to prolonged depression. Although it is the opposite, mental filtering has the same negative outcomes as overgeneralization.

In mental filtering, a person considers one small event and focuses on it exclusively, filtering out anything else—unlike overgeneralization, where a person considers one small event and generalizes the same outcome onto upcoming situations.

Limitations of Mental Filtering

As the name indicates, the mental filter forces a person to only filter out the positive and focus on negative thoughts and patterns. This negative mindset can have a detrimental impact on a person's well-being.

The mental filter is a type of distortion which results in several cognitive or behavioral issues such as anxiety, lack of self-confidence, interpersonal problems, and drug abuse.

Mental Disturbance Associated with Mental Filtering

Long-term negative thoughts can lead to hopelessness and an increased risk of suicidal thinking.

People with this cognitive distortion may lose their desire to live and develop the idea that ending one's life would be easier than facing everyday struggles.

Real-life Example

Amanda struggles with her married life because she focuses on all the harmful or hurtful things her partner has said or done while filtering out all the kind and loving gestures. This negative mental filter prevents Amanda from building a strong relationship with her spouse.

47

Discounting the Positive

Discounting the positive is a cognitive distortion where an individual does not appreciate the bright side of life. Such thinking involves invalidating the good things and rejecting the happy moments in your life. It is somewhat similar to mental filtering, but someone with this thinking pattern not only ignores the positives but also actively rejects them.

Limitations of Discounting the Positive

Positive events are viewed as a fluke when people experience this cognitive distortion.

The positive events are considered anomalies, which the individual presumes are rare events and something not likely to happen again in their life. Discounting the positive makes you question your potential and abilities. You attribute your success to good luck and refuse to recognize your skill, strengths, and competency.

The Mental Impact of Discounting the Positive

When you discount the positive and then need to face

a challenging situation, you will doubt your ability to cope with the stressor. This lack of self-belief will create depression and learned helplessness where you come to the wrong conclusion in your mind that there is no benefit in making an effort to improve the situation.

Real-life Example

Adam gave a presentation on the International Financial Reporting System and received an award of appreciation for his excellent illustration. Instead of carrying a feeling of accomplishment, Adam attributes the reward to sheer luck, which has nothing to do with his hard work toward the task.

Jumping to Conclusions

This type of cognitive distortion shows up in two ways—mind-reading and fortune-telling.

Mind Reading

Mind reading is a type of cognitive distortion where a person assumes that someone will act in a particular manner, assuming with a gut feeling rather than basing their beliefs on real experiences. Mind reading also involves imagining things other people might think, which is often not the case in reality.

Fortune-telling

Fortune telling is a cognitive distortion that involves having a mindset that predicts that events will unfold in a particular way. People often make this type of prediction of future events to avoid situations that are difficult for them to deal with.

The Mental Impact of Jumping to Conclusions

Jumping to conclusions means that a person is living in a created world of fake scenarios and lies. Such people are unable to realize their situation. They find it challenging to accept real-life situations, causing them to be anxious and incapable of dealing with stressful situations.

Real-life Example

Loraine engaged in fortune-telling when she assumed that she would not be able to go through life without the use of prohibited drugs. She believed in a self-prediction that heroin would sustain her in the long run if she wanted to live happily. In reality, after therapy, she realized that she could live a stress-free life without drug dependency.

Magnification

Magnification involves lessening the importance of desirable qualities essential to one's personality and exaggerating the extent of one's problems and shortcomings. This cognitive distortion is somewhat similar to the negative thinking patterns experienced in mental filtering and discounting the positive. It is defined as magnifying negative traits and qualities while minimizing positive ones.

Limitations of Magnification

People who use magnification patterns of thinking presume that other people notice, observe, and judge their every move and manipulate their minor mistakes. Such a state of fear keeps the person imprisoned in a cage of anxiety which may later take other forms.

Individuals doubt their abilities and coping

mechanisms to deal with stressful situations. Their self-doubt further triggers anxiety levels and deteriorates overall mental health.

The Mental Impact of Magnification

Magnification can affect an individual's behavioral and mental well-being in various ways. It contributes to emotional instability and triggers feelings of anxiety, fear, and panic.

These cognitive distortions destroy the lives of healthy people by exaggerating the importance of insignificant problems. As a result, a person suffering from magnified negative thinking stays unhappy and depressed.

Real-life Example

Jordan is addicted to the consumption of pain-killer medicines. He magnifies how important it is to eliminate and minimize bodily aches and exaggerates how unbearable his pain is.

Emotional Reasoning

Emotional reasoning is a cognitive distortion in which people judge themselves and situations based on strong, personal emotions. Emotional reasoning can have long-lasting impacts on the self-esteem of an individual.

This emotional pattern may lead someone to believe that they are a terrible person if they have feelings of guilt. The normal emotion of guilt related to a past event can become an alarming level of depression if one makes the situation worse with negative emotional reasoning.

Limitations of Emotional Reasoning

Emotional reasoning deceives and, in some ways, lies to a person. It makes a person believe that if their inner experience or feeling toward a situation is negative, then the actual situation must also be negative. Emotional reasoning hinders the accurate depiction of reality as one relies on their emotions.

The Mental Impact of Emotional Reasoning

Several mental problems arise in those who adopt the habit of negative emotional reasoning. The most common ones are anxiety and depression. Moreover, this distortion is a common way of thinking that many people engage in. We sometimes consider it normal and assume that someone who does not possess this type of thinking is not a cheerful or lively person.

Real-life Example

After being rejected by a few girls in her new college, Rachel uses emotional reasoning to conclude that she is a worthless person. Such negative thinking makes her anxious and leads her to adopt overeating habits and isolate herself from her social circles.

Labeling

When people label, they define themselves and others based on a single event or behavior. During labeling, people reduce themselves or others to a single, usually negative, characteristic or descriptor, like "drunk" or "failure."

Limitations of Labeling

Labeling usually involves judging ourselves or others for our behavior rather than seeing it as one characteristic. Although the behavior may not be desirable, it is just one trait that doesn't define us. Labeling involves attaching a title to someone which doesn't allow that person to be seen as anything else outside of that restrictive labeled box. It can be regarded as an extreme type of all-or-nothing thinking.

The Mental Impact of Labeling

The negative thinking pattern of labeling makes a person generally aggressive. The manipulative nature produced as a result of labeling induces feelings of stress in the person suffering from it.

Real-life Example

Based on your perception, you might label yourself and those around you as failures. You may decide that a person is a "loser" because of just one incident and continue judging them through that label for all future interactions. There is no likelihood that the negative label for oneself or the other person can be easily altered.

Should Statements

As the name indicates, "should" statements are cognitive patterns of thinking that make you think about what you *should* do or things you *must* do. These statements make you feel anxious or worried during the day and sleepless at night.

Limitations of Should Statements

These distortions cause misery and a sense of failure. Because of the constant cognitive pressure that you or others should be doing something, you feel like a failure in every situation. Even though your list includes what others should and shouldn't do or how they should behave, blaming yourself for what they should or shouldn't have done (but didn't) can increase stress and anxiety. You will never be happy if you always focus on what should (or shouldn't) have been done or said.

The Mental Impact of Should Statements

Should statements are the self-defeating ways we address ourselves and set unattainable goals. By creating such high standards beyond our control, we ultimately find ourselves defeated in our own eyes, having fallen short of our ideas and plans. This cognitive distortion results in anxiety, panic attacks, and sleeplessness.

Real-life Example

Solomon thinks he should play guitar easily without making any errors. However, when he makes a mistake while playing the guitar, he gets furious and upset. As a result, he starts to avoid practicing the guitar.

Personalization and Blame

Personalization and blame is a cognitive distortion in which you blame yourself or another person for a situation involving many uncontrollable factors.

Limitations of Personalization and Blame

Personalization leads to persistent sadness and constantly feeling that you are not enough to succeed in a given situation. Blame involves passing judgment on other people while ignoring the facts that might have been the cause of the problematic situation.

The Mental Impact of Personalization and Blame

This cognitive pattern causes people to feel insufficient in many aspects of their lives. People also experience feelings of shame, guilt, isolation, and depression when they keep blaming themselves or others.

Real-life Examples

Veronica blames herself for not being a good mother since her daughter's school grades have gone down. Instead of looking at the situation objectively and finding out if her child faces any other problems, she begins accusing herself for this academic failure.

One might blame the problems of a relationship on the spouse while closing their eyes to their own role in creating conflicts and weakening the bond.

<u>Catastrophizing</u>

Catastrophizing occurs when we assume that something worse will happen. It involves believing that we are in a very grave situation, when we are actually exaggerating the problem. Research shows that people who are often fatigued are more likely to catastrophize.

People with this cognitive distortion may have alterations in their pituitary and hypothalamus responses and increased activity in other parts of the brain responsible for dealing with pain-related emotions.

Limitations of Catastrophizing

Catastrophizing has a strong connection to generalized fatigue. Catastrophizing starts as a small thought which eventually turns into more considerable stress, inducing a state of panic. This multiplied stress may appear as physical signs of muscular pain, headache, etc. It can also result in uncontrollable emotional instability, manifesting as panic attacks.

The Mental Impact of Catastrophizing

People who catastrophize are often caught up in depression and various anxiety disorders such as generalized anxiety disorder (GAD), obsessive-compulsive disorder (OCD), and post-traumatic stress disorder (PTSD).

Real-life Example

You might develop negative self-talk regarding a criticism your employer gave you. You then start to assume that he may fire you. Multiplying one thought with another, you may start worrying about how you will find a good job again. You then experience extreme depression by imagining yourself economically down and homeless.

Perfectionism

Perfectionism is a combination of overcritical self-evaluations and high personal standards. It comes in three forms: self-oriented, other-oriented, and socially prescribed perfectionism.

Limitations of Perfectionism

Individuals may attach irrational importance to perfection and hold unrealistic expectations of themselves and others.

The Mental Impact of Perfectionism

Anxiety, depression, suicidal thoughts, and bipolar disorder are a few mental problems faced by those who adopt the distortive mindset of perfectionism.

Perfectionism is also linked with eating disorders that result from an over-conscious mind. Also, clinical depression and premature deaths are recorded among students and young people who had been in the trap of perfectionism. Perfectionism is often instilled in people at a young age or in students in school, particularly if they are the oldest child in their family or due to their culture. This is one of the most complex cognitive distortions to combat because it is so ingrained in people from a young age and usually done so to either "get the best grades," "bring honor to your family," "get that high-paying job," or "move away from the worse situation." But, perfectionism is an illusion that most people can't see through.

Real-life example

Adam perceives that his elite social circle is highly demanding, and his friends might judge him harshly—

therefore, he must display perfection to secure approval.

Procrastination

Procrastination is the act of delaying tasks until the last minute or past the deadline. It is a self-regulation failure in which a person becomes lethargic despite the potentially harmful consequences.

Limitations of Procrastination

One crucial drawback to procrastination is that we need to feel motivated or inspired to start a job or a project. We hold ourselves back from taking the initiative by drawing such assumptions.

In some cases, procrastination is not just poor time management. It has become a significant part of people's lifestyles. It then affects life in terms of financial, social, and mental well-being. Procrastinating and worrying about what you need to do takes energy, on top of the energy it takes actually to do the task, and can lead you to act reactively, forcing you to scramble to catch up.

The Mental Impact of Procrastination

Depression is often associated with procrastination since such a state keeps an individual hopeless and doubtful of ever accomplishing a goal to the fullest.

Also, procrastination is common in obsessive-compulsive disorder patients. These people remain in a general state of fear—fear of performing a task correctly and anxiety over new mistakes. The "undesirable" task is scary for multiple reasons: because most people don't want to ask for help, they might make mistakes, or they might actually succeed and be expected to perform just as well for the next project.

Real-life Example

Ralph had committed to completing an art project over the weekend, but instead, he spent his time watching the soccer match. In this way, he delayed what was necessary while following trivial pursuits.

63

How Can We Influence Our Feelings?

There are several ways to reshape our feelings after a difficult situation. One negative thought can add to another, which leads to the multiplication of stress and increased depression. Without our knowledge, we become a victim of negative thinking patterns. We must realize the importance of emotional health and how it can impact us in every possible manner.

The following are some ways we can regain our power of positivity and alleviate stress:

Positive Self-talk

What we feed to our minds affects our overall being. Our self-talk must always be motivating. Degrading words that we say to ourselves diminishes confidence and lessens our ability to flourish. A positive mindset contributes toward changing the ways we perceive a situation. Even if it sounds "outdated" or "cheesy," an affirmation or helpful saying that you can use to pump yourself up every day is beneficial. Use favorite quotations, put them throughout your house where you can see them, and say them often. Although, current research suggests that positive self-talk is less about motivating ourselves than about being aware of our actual feelings, seeing/hearing the negative self-talk, and finding ways to invalidate that way of thinking about ourselves.

Developing Willpower

Negative thinking and stressful situations can leave a person feeling hopeless, losing the desire to take the initiative on many tasks. For example, if you had previously thought something was difficult for you to learn, you can develop willpower and influence your feelings by telling yourself that learning is gradual. And slowly, with self-motivation, you can overcome your doubts.

Keep Good Company

The people we spend time with play a significant role in shaping our feelings. It will add negative thoughts to our minds if our companions are de-motivating. Being with the right people will keep us happy and keep our minds off unnecessary stress. Amit Goldenberg and his team of researchers found that the people you surround yourself with will infinitely influence your emotions and feelings: "It seems that the best way to regulate your emotions is to start with the selection of your environment," Goldenberg said. "If you don't want to be angry today, one way to do that is to avoid angry people. Do some people have an ingrained preference for stronger emotions than others? That's one of my next questions" (qtd. in Shashkevich).

Choose Wisely

When we are careful about our long-term decisions, we contribute to our overall health. People must be comfortable at their residence, workplace, or other institution. Your environment will impact your thoughts—therefore, it is in your hands which environment you choose for yourself to always have a happy mindset.

Talk to a Healthcare Provider

Negative patterns of thinking can alter one's sense of reality. If your negative thoughts are having an impact on your relationships, work-life, and goals, you should seek the help of a therapist or a healthcare provider.

These professionals provide step-by-step guidance for overcoming negative thinking.

Try Cognitive Behavioral Therapy

Cognitive-behavioral therapy, or CBT, effectively overcomes many cognitive distortions by assisting an individual in recognizing and learning the ways real-life situations should be handled. It is a goal-oriented, problem-solving psychotherapy treatment. It focuses on current problems and finding coping mechanisms for those problems.

This therapy helps individuals understand that failure or success should not be treated as an extreme black-and-white concept. When negative thoughts are addressed, self-defeating thoughts are replaced with positive, motivational thoughts, and you feel better about your strengths and ability to proceed in life.

Use Graded Exposure

Graded exposure involves identifying anxiety-provoking situations, developing a hierarchy, and planning exposures. Exposure therapy is behavior-addressing therapy designed to assist people in managing their fears.

Graded exposure aims to improve the quality of life for an individual by creating an acceptance of dreaded situations and reducing anxiety levels by allowing them to face their fears. Systematic desensitization is one of the widely used methods of graded exposure. Relaxation techniques are applied during exposure to the ranked items of fear to offset stress and anxiety.

Graded exposure is beneficial in treating various cognitive distortions, including overgeneralization, procrastination, perfectionism, and catastrophizing.

It is also effective in treating certain mental disorders such as OCD. The defects in personality caused by negative mental patterns can permanently impact an individual and those around them. Accepting help from therapies is highly recommended to help gain new insight.

Meditation and Mindfulness

Meditation and mindfulness have also proven to be an effective treatment for stress. Mindfulness means being present in the moment and in your body, and paying attention to the things that we would typically rush through. Mindfulness is about turning down the volume in your mind and returning to your body, focusing on the events and things happening right now. Meditation and mindfulness exercises usually use focused breathing exercises to help. However, this is not always necessary.

Deep abdominal breathing increases the supply of oxygen to your brain and promotes a feeling of calmness. Deep breathing helps activate the body's relaxation response and studies show that abdominal breathing for 20 to 30 minutes daily reduces anxiety and stress. Deep abdominal increases the supply of oxygen to your brain and promotes a feeling of calmness. The next time you're feeling anxious try this simple relaxation technique:

1. Place one hand on your chest and the other on your abdomen. Inhale slowly and deeply through your nose. Keep your shoulders

relaxed. Your abdomen should expand, and your chest should rise very little.

2.   Exhale slowly through your mouth. As you blow air out, purse your lips slightly, but keep your jaw relaxed.

3.   Repeat this breathing exercise for several minutes.

Know Your Ability to Fight Stress

We do not have to control every aspect of our lives. Too much consciousness over things and situations makes us anxious.

You can feel better about things by adopting a positive pattern of thoughts. Know that you have control over your life—you are the decision-maker who can choose a happy or sad life for yourself.

Sometimes we exhaust ourselves by trying to control the uncontrollable events in our lives. We should appreciate the positive traits that help us cope with everyday struggles and accept that there will be times when things will be beyond our control. Every level of life will demand patience and a positive outlook. Even just a few healthy changes in our routine can help us alleviate stress levels. These changes include exercising, positive daily goals, meditation, self-appreciation, etc.

Address Your Mind

Often people experience a control fallacy—that is, a notion that you can control or you need to control more than your actual capacity to manage things. You should identify your thought patterns to realize that they are not always rational, and your mind might be deceiving you into overthinking. Therefore, addressing one's mind is vital to direct your thinking patterns in the correct direction.

Know What You Can Control and What You Cannot Control

Identifying what you can control will often help you realize things that are not in your hands. This realization will help you do what you can and surrender the rest. As a result, unnecessary mental pressure gets settled, and you will experience peace of mind.

Focus On Yourself, Your Behavior, and Your Thoughts to Shape Your Routine

Put your energy into more productive tasks instead of losing power over uncontrollable stressors. Uncontrollable events impact our lives, but our happiness depends on our ability to deal with the stress associated with that sudden event in a wise manner.

We should also accept the fact that life is always not fair. There will be positive as well as negative situations. Living to the fullest in happy moments and addressing the bad moments with a positive mindset will help us be truly at peace.

An unexpected accident or a natural calamity is not under our control. Such situations require accepting and dealing with the stressor as positively as possible. Also, what other people think, feel, or say is beyond our control—expecting others to behave the way we want will leave us sad and disappointed. Letting go of unmanageable conditions leads to peace, happiness, freedom, and serenity.

CHAPTER 3: STRESS AND ITS EFFECT ON OUR BODY

"Stress acts as an accelerator: it will push you either forward or backward, but you choose which direction." —Chelsea Erieau

Stress and Cortisol

Whenever we confront a difficult situation, we feel a need for an extra boost of energy. Our brain detects such requirements, which prepares the entire body to respond to stress. When our body perceives the stress, our adrenal gland composes and regulates the stress

75

hormone cortisol in our bloodstream. This hormone activates our fight-or-flight response, which becomes evident by the increase in our heart rate and blood pressure.

An Optimum Cortisol Level

A balanced cortisol level is mandatory for survival, and it has kept humans alive and motivated to live for thousands of years. The normal cortisol levels are released and regulated in our bodies every morning as we wake up. Cortisol is also released as we exercise, positively impacting the body, which we see as the result of workouts and physical training.

These levels are essential for the overall health of the human body as they strengthen the heart and contribute to the regulation of blood pressure and sugar levels. The balance in sugar levels and blood pressure is vital to ensure a long healthy life.

When cortisol is available to the body in small amounts, it can provide numerous benefits such as strengthening memory, boosting the immune system, and reducing sensitivity to pain.

What Happens to the Body if Cortisol Levels Are High?

Cortisol levels begin to lower and eventually become normal as the body overcomes the stressor. However, if the body is always in high gear and in a state of elevated stress, it might constantly release the cortisol stress hormone, which can threaten health in the long run.

High Cortisol Levels

The following physiological changes will likely occur if cortisol levels are very high:

Impact on the Digestive System

When the body responds to a stressful situation, vital functions shut down or are suppressed during that time period. The digestive system is one critical function that is switched off while dealing with the stressor. If phases of high stress are constant, it will pose serious pressure on the digestive tract. As a result, the digestive system will not be able to process and absorb food well.

Patients with ulcers often report having high stress

levels. There is better symptom control when mental pressure is reduced. A stress-free mind aids in a speedy recovery. Other problems associated with the digestive system, such as colitis and irritable bowel syndrome, can be managed conveniently by lowering stress levels.

Impact on the Immune System

Normal cortisol levels are vital for keeping the immune system balanced. This hormone induces a healing impact on the body by reducing inflammation in times of illness.

However, a rise in cortisol levels suppresses the function of the immune system. This makes it difficult to fight any minor illness or even a disease.

A weak immune system would easily fall prey to allergies, colds, digestive problems, and contagious infections. Also, with increased cortisol levels in the body for extended periods, there is an increased risk of chronic diseases, including autoimmune digestive disorders and cancer.

Impact on Body Weight

Cortisol also increases the appetite. It tells the body to fill energy stores with energy-dense foods and carbs, causing us to crave comfort foods. A high cortisol level can also cause us to put on those extra calories as visceral or deep belly fat. This type of fat does not just make us overweight. It actively releases hormones and immune system chemicals called cytokines that increase your chances of developing chronic diseases, like heart disease and insulin resistance.

Understanding the cravings caused by high cortisol levels is essential as they can directly impact your health. When your cells cry out for the provision of energy, your body sends messages to the brain to create a feeling of hunger and a rising requirement that you need to eat. There is a close association between the cortisol levels in the body and the amount of calorie intake. False signals to eat more and fill your hunger will make you crave a high-calorie diet, which might be appealing to the eye, or the taste buds, but remains dangerous for your health. This results in the accumulation of stored carbohydrates in the form of fats and unused glucose, which usually needs to be utilized by the body for instant energy.

Impact on Cardiovascular Health

Cortisol causes the endothelium, or blood vessels' inner lining, not to function normally. Scientists now know this is the early step leading to cholesterol plaque buildup in arteries. Together these changes increase your chance of heart attack or stroke.

How to Detect Cortisol Levels

If you experience signs and symptoms of chronic stress, you should visit a medical practitioner. A simple saliva test will help detect your cortisol levels. Once high stress hormone levels are identified, the doctor can provide you with a detailed plan to subsidize your stress and balance the cortisol levels. A well-executed program of changing your routine and adopting healthy practices will relieve your stressful mind and, in turn, contribute to your physical health.

Stressors

What Is a Stressor?

A stressor is an event or an external stimulus that the

mind and body perceive as dangerous or harmful. The stressor can be a chemical or biological agent which causes stress to an individual and induces feelings of uncertainty. A person might find themself struggling and pressured in the presence of a stressor. Not everyone responds to stressors in the same way because of differences in perception. What might be stressful for one individual may not be necessarily stressful for another.

Types of Stressors

It is important to note that stressors are not necessarily negative. There are positive stressors that help a person stay motivated and keep moving. Some stressors which we experience in our day-to-day lives include the following:

Financial Stressors

Financial stressors induce stress related to money problems, such as unpaid bills, taxes, unplanned expenses, meeting deadlines at work, legal issues, bankruptcy, etc.

Personal or Relationship Stressors

This type of stressor can result in positive changes for an individual. Positive stressors falling into this category include marriage, the birth of a child, moving, taking a vacation, arrival of the holiday season, etc.

Personal stressors can induce short or long-term negative impacts on a person's life. Examples include an accident, hospitalization, separation from a spouse or other close family member, conflicts in relationships, death of a loved one, dealing with children's problems at school, injury, being abused or neglected, or loss of contact with a close friend or family member.

Organizational Stressors

Organizational stressors can be positive, including pressure to get a good grade or a positive force to achieve a work goal. Receiving bonuses, promotions, and praise at work and starting a new task will provide reasonable remuneration as desirable motivation. Small amounts of stress to meet deadlines in the workplace are considered healthy as it allows for inspiration and an intention to continuously mold and

82

improve oneself.

However, these stressors can also be harmful, including restrictive and overly rigid rules and regulations at one's workplace, aggressive work culture, anxiety about performance, etc. Such stressors make a person less efficient and deteriorate their ability to work.

Relative Stressors

Relative stressors carry different intensities and meanings for different individuals since the way humans perceive a threat is unique for all. These stressors are subjective and may result in varying levels of stress. They may result in a calm response from some people and a violent reaction from others. Examples include attempting an exam, getting stuck in traffic, and changes in labor hours at the workplace.

Absolute Stressors

The majority of individuals feel stressed when exposed to absolute stressors. These are objective or universal stressors beyond human control and are dominated by natural forces. Examples include earthquakes, floods, hurricanes, etc.

Lifestyle Stressors

This category includes those stressors that are related to the way we live. If we have poor habits, they will increase our stress levels and destroy our health. Not getting enough sleep, lack of a healthy diet, alcohol and drug consumption, and too much caffeine are some lifestyle stressors that slowly steal the happiness from our lives.

Environmental Stressors

Environmental stressors may impact our physical as well as psychological health. What we receive from our environment can highly affect our stress levels. Such stressors include noise pollution, bright lights that irritate our eyes, and discomfort due to environmental temperature, which can be excessive cold or heat.

Acute vs. Chronic Stress

Acute Stress

Acute stress is another name for short-term stress that triggers one's fight-or-flight response, and the body is brought back to its normal state of calmness as soon as the stressor has been dealt with. Examples include short-term illness and minor difficulties in daily routine, such as a car running out of gas.

Acute stress results from specific events and situations that generally last for a definite time. These events may involve unpredictability, a threat to one's ego, temporary uncertainty, novelty, etc. Acute stress is isolated to the present situation or an incident that imparts stress on an individual and does not relate to any other event. Therefore, we can presume acute stress to be an on-the-spot type of stress.

Whenever you are experiencing an acute type of stress, your symptoms could be one or more of the following:

- Raised heart rate
- Anxiety

- Sweating
- Chest pain
- Shortness of breath

Acute stress can be considered good for you as stress hormones are released for a limited time to equip your mind and body to deal with stressful situations. A peaceful state follows the brief form of high energy as the threatening situation gets under control or the problem is completely resolved.

Examples of acute stress include overcoming a car accident, being called to make a public speech, etc. Such experiences alert you to seize the moment and feel pumped up. This indicates that your stress hormones provide a solid backup to handle challenging situations.

Chronic Stress

Chronic stress is long-term or ongoing in nature and gradually builds up when there are more extended periods of stressful situations in one's life. Once chronic stress gets hold of a person, it can seriously damage both physical and mental health. Persistent experiences of chronic stress will lead to high blood

86

pressure, high cholesterol, and autoimmune diseases such as diabetes. The long-term effects of chronic stress can leave a person in a disturbed state of mind. In extreme cases, they may become an addict or remain depressed and anxious most of the time.

As you pass through persistent phases of chronic stress, your symptoms could include one or more of the following:

- Depression
- General unhappiness
- Anxiety
- Agitation
- Moodiness
- Irritability
- Anger
- Loneliness
- Isolation

Our stress response system is not designed to be constantly activated. Since chronic stress forces the body to stay alert to cope with the situation, it leads to wear and tear on our body and mental health. It is advisable to always seek help in cases of chronic stress.

Simple talk therapy can help as you can share your heart with a close friend or a family member. Chronic stress can be managed by adopting a healthy lifestyle, maintaining a balanced diet, exercising regularly, and ensuring the right amount of rest and sleep.

If these do not help improvise your condition, you will need to have chronic stress treated under the supervision of a medical practitioner. This treatment is crucial to your mental health as it will help relieve the burden and enable you to switch to a stress-free lifestyle.

Causes of Stress

Almost anything can cause stress, depending on the situation and your ability to cope with it. Stress is an unavoidable reality that ranges from less severe conditions to more significant events. Many factors and situations become causes of stress for an individual. The level of influence of a particular situation is unique for every person. Here are some common conditions that may induce stress:

Job and Workplace

Deadlines, challenging bosses, troublesome colleagues, office politics, even harassment and discrimination in the workplace—all these things can keep you awake at night with worry and fear. Your job is a big part of your daily life. When things aren't going well, stress at work can mount. On the other hand, if you're unemployed, stress factors may be related to loss of income and basic necessities such as food and shelter.

Finances

Looming bills, credit card debt, bill collectors, identity theft and fraud, and even the act of checking your savings account balance can all inspire stress. For most people, money is a necessity. Some people struggle to make ends meet, and others are unemployed or underemployed. Worries may swirl around how to buy groceries, pay the electric bill, pay the doctor's bill, and how to pay the rent or mortgage. The downstream effects of stress can make surviving and thriving even more challenging.

Disasters and Trauma

Natural or man-made disasters and traumatic events can significantly impact someone's life. Tornadoes, wildfires, hurricanes, and flooding can lead to loss of life, home, and community. This kind of stress can become overwhelming. The stress of traumatic events, like being the victim of an attack or a serious accident, can lead to deep and long-lasting stress and health issues.

Relationships and Family

Children, divorce, separation, loneliness, and even the responsibility of caring for a family can have stressful impacts. Stress also plays a significant role in health and wellness for those dealing with the death of a loved one, sickness, or having to be a caregiver for an ill or elderly family member.

Effects of Stress

If you tend to feel stressed regularly, your body may exist in an elevated state of stress. And that can lead to serious health problems. Chronic stress disrupts nearly every system in the body. It can suppress the immune system, upset the digestive and reproductive systems, increase the risk of heart attack and stroke, and speed up the aging process. It can even rewire the brain, leaving you more vulnerable to anxiety, depression, and other mental health problems.

Health problems caused or exacerbated by stress may include:

- Depression and anxiety
- Headaches
- Insomnia or sleep problems
- Autoimmune diseases
- Digestive problems
- Skin conditions such as eczema
- Heart disease
- Weight problems
- Reproductive issues
- Memory issues
- Colds, flu, viruses, and other illnesses
- Fatigue
- Irritability and anger
- Substance use

Stress can affect our behavioral, emotional, and physical health. It is essential to recognize how stress affects different aspects of our lives and learn coping abilities to fight these stressors. Following are some effects of stress found in relationships, social life, physical problems, and the workplace.

Relationship Stress

- Lack of communication
- Loss of intimacy
- Dominance or control of one spouse over the other
- Feelings of insecurity

Social Stress

- Preferring social isolation
- Increased level of frustration toward others
- Less patience to tolerate others
- Difficulty maintaining a social circle

Physiological Stress

- Fatigue
- Heart palpitations

- Muscle tension
- Digestive issues and illnesses such as gastroenteritis

Workplace Stress

- Lack of creativity
- Disinterest
- Decreased punctuality
- Increased sick leaves
- Poor work performance

Burnout

People struggling to cope with stress may be at high risk of *burnout*. Herbert Freudenberger coined the term *burnout* in 1974. In 2019, the World Health Organization (WHO) officially classified it as a medical diagnosis, including the condition in its *International Classification of Diseases*. This handbook guides medical providers in diagnosing diseases. It describes burnout as "a syndrome conceptualized as resulting from chronic workplace stress that has not been successfully managed."

Burnout can leave people feeling exhausted, empty, and unable to cope with the demands of life. Burnout may be accompanied by various mental and physical health symptoms as well. If left unaddressed, burnout can make it difficult for individuals to function well in their daily lives.

Burnout is not a condition that happens suddenly—it evolves over time. If left untreated, stress develops into chronic stress and eventually crosses over into burnout. Stress makes people feel that they have too much on their plate, but burnout makes them feel depleted—like they have nothing else left to give.

Individuals experiencing burnout commonly use phrases such as "I'm in survival mode," "I'm exhausted," "I've had enough," or "I'm done."

Physical signs of burnout are similar to those of stress. They include fatigue, insomnia, changes in appetite, tenseness in the body, and an increased rate of illness. Some of the emotional and behavioral symptoms are irritability, sarcasm, debilitating self-doubt or self-criticism, lack of motivation, procrastination, isolation, and loss of enjoyment in life. You may be on the road to burnout if you begin to make these statements or have these feelings:

- *Every* day is a bad day.

- Caring about your work or home life seems like a total waste of energy.

- You're exhausted all the time.

- The majority of your day is spent on tasks you find either mind-numbingly dull or overwhelming.

- You feel like nothing you do makes a difference or is appreciated.

While burnout may be the result of stress, it is not the same as too much stress. Stress overwhelming involves *too much*. Too much pressure that demands too much physically and mentally. In spite of this, people under stress generally see a positive end of stress if they are able to get things under control. In contrast, burnout involves too little or not enough—feeling empty and devoid of motivation, beyond caring, and an extremely pessimistic view of their future.

CHAPTER 4: IDENTIFYING THE SOURCES OF STRESS IN YOUR LIFE

"Times of stress are also times that are signals for growth, and if we use adversity properly, we can grow through adversity." —**Rabbi Dr. Abraham Twerski**

Identify Your Stressors

Recognizing the sources of stress is the first step toward managing stress. When we desperately need relief from our stress levels, we must first identify the root cause of stress instead of jumping to the solutions.

Different stressors impose different levels of strain on an individual and demand a unique way to be dealt with.

Acute stress is short-term and can be recognized easily by noticing the events related to a specific period. For instance, your inbox is overflowing with emails about your pending work, or you cannot meet the deadlines, and you are scared of your boss' reaction. Such stressors do not harm an individual as one achieves a state of relaxation when the stressor is managed, and the task is completed.

However, there are times when an individual experiences long-term depression in the shape of acute or chronic stress. Such situations require a serious call to treatment. When we cannot recognize symptoms of stress, it may lead to health problems such as diabetes, high blood pressure, heart problems, digestive problems, etc.

Stressors can take a heavy toll, beginning with minor mood changes. Therefore, identifying the stressors is crucial. The warning signs that appear as the

98

consequence of stress are as follows:

Effect on Cognition

Cognitive disturbances caused by stress include lack of concentration, negative racing thoughts, negative or anxious mind, poor judgment, constant worrying, and trouble remembering things.

Effect on Emotions

Emotional instability due to stress includes general anxiety and depression, agitation, social isolation, irritability, and feelings of being overwhelmed.

Effect on Physical Health

Stress's physical impacts include increased allergies, chest pain, a burden on the heart, dizziness, nausea, diarrhea, constipation, and loss of sex drive.

Effect on Behavior

Behavioral disturbances caused by stress include social withdrawal; nervous habits such as nail-biting and pacing; use of drugs such as cigarettes, anti-depressants, and relaxants; increased consumption of alcohol; procrastinating; and neglecting responsibilities.

Assess Your Stressors

We encounter a variety of stressors every day. It is essential to understand what type of stressor you are facing to prepare yourself to deal with it in the safest way possible. Following is a list of stressors through which you can perform a self-assessment to determine how much stress affects your overall well-being.

	STRESSOR	LOW-IMPACT	MEDIUM-IMPACT	HIGH-IMPACT
1	Injury or illness	-	-	-
2	Death of a loved one	-	-	-
3	Problems at the workplace	-	-	-

4	Relationship conflicts	-	-	-
5	Legal issues	-	-	-
6	Financial instability	-	-	-
7	An unexpected event	-	-	-

Calculate Your Stress Score

The Social Readjustment Rating Scale (SRRS), also known as Holmes and Rahe Stress Scale, is an assessment scale to manage stress before it causes severe damage to our physical and mental health.

Holmes and Rahe (1967) found a positive relationship between life changes and an individual's illness. This scale was designed to assess one's response to most common life stressors. By summing up the impact of

101

various stressors, one can determine the intensity of stress levels and compare it with the three ranges of scores provided with this stress management scale.

Scoring on SRRS

Less Than 150

A total score of 150 or less indicates a low level of stress and a very low probability of developing a stress-related disorder.

Between 150 and 300

A total score of 150 to 299 suggests a moderate stress level, and the possibility of developing a stress-related disorder increases up to 50%.

300 or Above

If your score is 300 or more (up to 600), that suggests a high stress level, and the chances of developing a stress-related disorder are about 80%.

STRESSORS	IMPACT SCORE
Death of spouse	100
Divorce	76
Marital separation	65
Jail term	63
Death of close family member	63
Personal injury or illness	53
Marriage	50
Fired at work	47
Marital reconciliation	45
Retirement	45
Change in health of family member	44
Pregnancy	40
Sex difficulties	39
Business readjustment	39
Gain of a new family member	39
Change in financial status	38
Death of a companion	37
Change in occupation	36
Change in amount of arguments w/ spouse	35
Major mortgage	31

Foreclosure of mortgage or loan	30
Change in responsibilities at work	29
Separation from a family member	29
Trouble maintaining relationships	29
Personal achievement	28
Beginning or end of a job	26
Beginning or end of schooling	26
Change in living conditions	25
Change in personal habits	24
Trouble with one's employer	23
Fluctuations in work hours or conditions	20
Moving to a new home	20
Change in schooling	20
Change in recreational activities	19
Change in physical activities	19
Change in routine	19
Matters of mortgage or loan	17
Change in sleeping habits	16
Change in social circle	15
Change in eating habits	15
Vacation	13
Annual meetings	12

Theft or law violation	11

How Do You Respond to Stressful Situations?

An individual must know their abilities and limits concerning stress management. Tools such as SRRS prove helpful for a person when they experience a stressful situation and want to address the problem. Also, how one utilizes the fight-or-flight response to cope with the stressor impacts the effect on one's overall health.

You can respond to the stressor by the fight response generated by your adrenaline. Your body will feel highly energetic and boosted to fight the stressor for a while. However, the aggressive fight behavior to combat the stressful situation should be subsidized upon solving the matter. If our fight response stays persistent, it begins to deteriorate our health, which is undesirable. The increased cortisol levels in the fight response can be dangerous. Therefore, it is advisable to manage and deal with the stressors wisely.

Freeze or Flee Response

Certain scenarios do not require an aggressive reaction. In such cases, it is advisable to either flee from the stressor or take a flight from it. This will contribute to your physical and mental health. Stressors often become more intense if we fight back, but they will settle if we act with tolerance and patience. Choosing one's fight or flight response in the right way is essential to combat the stressors each day brings.

Managing Perceived Threats

The things that induce fear in us are perceived threats that differ for each person. The response we initiate toward the perceived threat is also unique, and the level of fear or anxiety can vary for each hazard. To choose the correct coping mechanisms, we need to identify which situations we consider dangerous in order to deal with threatening conditions.

Our body automatically generates the fight-or-flight response to protect us from what our brain perceives as dangerous or life-threatening.

After knowing your stress score, you will be able to see the amount of help you require to manage your stress levels. It is recommended to try avoiding a long-term aggressive response to stressful situations. If your stress response remains overactive, you must adopt effective strategies to achieve balance and regain mental health.

CHAPTER 5: PRACTICE THE 4 A'S

"Stress is not what happens to us. It's our response TO what happens. And RESPONSE is something we can choose." —**Maureen Killoran**

What is the 4 A's Approach?

Stress occurs when external stimuli upset an individual's natural equilibrium or homeostasis. In challenging circumstances, it is essential to adopt convenient methods to help relieve stress and live a life full of peace and contentment.

The 4 A's approach is an easy-to-understand technique

109

to cope with inevitable stressors and to learn to deal with stress in ways that provide long-term benefits. Following are four A's that can help any person deal with the stressful situations safely and effectively:

1. Avoid the situation
2. Alter the situation
3. Accept the situation
4. Adapt to the situation

1. **Avoiding the Situation**

Not every situation deserves a response. It is critical to avoid unnecessary stress where possible. When reacting to every little matter, we unintentionally exhaust ourselves. Attempting tasks beyond our normal capacity automatically induces a feeling of depression in our brain. There are many stressors that we encounter daily. We should realize that we have control over these stressors, and we can avoid or eliminate them to achieve balance in our life.

Trim Your To-do List

It is crucial to analyze daily tasks, responsibilities, and schedules and know how to prioritize your work. When you can identify that your workload is too heavy, you can lessen your burden by either keeping the unnecessary tasks at the end of your to-do list or eliminating them from your routine.

Learn How to Say No

There are many situations where we become confused about the timely management of things. We can feel relieved by realizing what needs to be done and which things can be avoided. It is not mandatory to say yes to everything and feel guilty for not fulfilling those commitments. Learning when to say no can keep you safe from mental pressure and overburdening yourself with responsibilities beyond your strength. For example, if you are overwhelmed at work, but your boss wants you to take on a new project, you might be tempted to just take the project, heightening your stress levels and deepening your unhappiness at your job. Yet, you do have a choice. By talking to your boss, and telling him that you are actually overwhelmed and that the new project would put you behind, you may be able to delegate some other projects to others who can handle the extra work, while you tackle the new project.

Avoid People Who Cause You Stress

Keeping a safe distance from those who become the cause of your stress can help relieve a lot of tension. For instance, if your coworker bothers you regularly, you can keep a safe physical distance from him. You can avoid unnecessary meetings with him until there is nothing critical to discuss or conduct with him.

Take Control of Your Environment

Take control over everyday stressors by adopting ways you can minimize your mental pressure. You should know that you have power over your surroundings. Instead of giving up on daily hardships, you should take one thing at a time and be careful not to burden yourself with unnecessary stressors.

2. <u>Altering the Situation</u>

If you can't avoid a stressful situation, try to alter it. This often involves changing how you communicate

112

and operate in your daily life.

Express Your Feelings

If the cause of stress is continuously a troublesome person, you can ask them to change their behavior. This little step can help you gain back a positive environment. Also, if someone complains about your behavior, you should take it positively and try to correct your attitude.

Communicate Clearly

It is essential to adopt a transparent and honest way of communicating in every part of your life, be it your personal relationships or your workplace. This habit can keep you safe from many troubles.

Manage Your Time Effectively

Create a balanced schedule. Try to balance work, family life, and social activities. If there are multiple tasks, you can group similar tasks to increase efficiency and spare some time for relaxation. Such changes can assist you in staying healthy and calm in the long run.

Set Boundaries

We encounter many challenging situations and people having different personalities every day. We should be careful that our problems do not become the reason for our anxiety. Therefore, before engaging in a difficult task or committing to a new person, you should clarify that you have limited time available—this will help you to avoid harsh results later.

3. __Accepting the Situation__

Don't try to control the uncontrollable. Accept the things you can't change. Some sources of stress are unavoidable. You can't prevent or change stressors such as the death of a loved one, a severe illness, or a pandemic. In such cases, the best way to cope with stress is to accept things as they are. Acceptance may be difficult, but it's easier than fighting against a situation you can't change.

Talk with Those Around You

When you discuss what's bothering you with others, it lessens the burden on your heart. Talking your heart out is a helpful method of getting over frustrating situations.

Be Forgiving

We live in an imperfect world, and people make mistakes. Let go of anger and resentments. Free yourself from negative energy by forgiving and moving on. Try to spend an entire week without complaining and see what a difference it makes.

Keep a Positive Mindset

Negative patterns of thinking can create an imbalance in one's health. However, if our self-talk is positive, it helps us regain confidence and allows us to maintain objectivity.

Grow From Your Failures

Mistakes are inevitable. We can positively use our flaws by considering them a lesson and trying to find something in them that will help our personal growth. It is okay, and even healthy, to realize that you cannot be 100% successful at everything all at once.

4. **Adapting to the Situation**

Adapting to a situation involves accepting the position and changing our perceptions and expectations. If you can't change the stressor, change yourself. Adjusting to the problem includes changing expectations and can help you be more optimistic and less stressed.

Adjust Your Standards

Perfectionism is a major source of avoidable stress. Stop setting yourself up for failure by demanding perfection. Set reasonable standards for yourself and others, and learn to be okay with being good enough rather than perfect. Perfectionism is also a creativity killer and prevents you and your team from exploring multiple options that you would never have investigated.

Reframe the Situation

When you look at a situation from a different perspective, it helps reduce anxiety levels. If you keep a positive outlook on bad situations, you can effectively manage the stressors. Try to view stressful situations from a more positive perspective. Rather than fuming about a traffic jam, look at it as an opportunity to pause and regroup, listen to your favorite radio station, sing that power ballad, or enjoy some alone time.

Focus on the Big Picture

When you look at the big picture to help prioritize things in life, you will release a large amount of stress from your life. Take a step back and assess your current situation. Ask yourself how important it will be in the long run. Will it matter in a month? A year? Is it worth getting upset over? If the answer is no, focus your time and energy elsewhere. Filtering unnecessary stress from the present can help you achieve contentment and peace of mind.

Positive Affirmations

Enchanting beautiful words that contribute to our health can help to relieve stress. When we repeat confident sentences in our minds, such as, "I am happy, healthy, and blessed," it can help keep our mood happy and jubilant throughout the day. It also helps to keep a record of your successes. Write down all the things that you have accomplished in a journal, or write them and put them in a jar to look back on

117

when things get hard. Writing down even small accomplishments and affirmations will help relieve stress.

Practice Gratitude

When stress is getting you down, take a moment to reflect on all the things you appreciate in your life, including your positive qualities and gifts.

CHAPTER 6: GET ACTIVE

Virtually any exercise, from aerobics to yoga, can act as a stress reliever. If you're not an athlete or even if you're out of shape, you can still make a little exercise go a long way toward stress management. Let's explore the connection between exercise and stress relief—and learn why exercise should be part of your stress management plan.

The Power of Movement

Many benefits of physical activity boost an individual's mind, body, and spirit. It is vital to understand that we should not exhaust ourselves beyond our physical

119

limit, nor become too lazy to seldom engage in physical tasks, which can make us sad and obese.

Physical activity as a key lifestyle factor plays a vital role in optimizing physical and emotional health. Physical activity provides innumerable benefits that even contribute to curing chronic diseases. People who add exercise to their routine are healthier, more energetic, and more optimistic than those who remain lethargic. Keeping one's body moving also adds motivation and a positive outlook to everyday situations.

Physical exercises, when conducted regularly, can recharge the body, lower our stress levels and also provide many other benefits, including the following:

- Promotion of self-healing
- Increased self-awareness
- Improved cognitive ability
- Increased focus and concentration and the ability to memorize things

- Activating the parasympathetic nervous system, which helps reduce stress and tension in the physical body
- Balances body weight
- Lowers blood cholesterol levels
- Increases blood circulation
- Prevents back pain
- Lowers the risk of cardiovascular disease
- Helps build stronger bones and increase bone mass, reducing the chances of osteoporosis
- Lowers blood pressure
- Decreases the risk of many diseases such as cancer, type 2 diabetes, etc.

Additional Benefits of Physical Activity

Mental Health

Physical activity induces a positive impact on one's mood, thus reducing symptoms of depression and anxiety.

Though a bit of stress is necessary to keep moving and

learning to succeed, it is crucial to keep the stress and anxiety caused by everyday situations at an equilibrium. This can be achieved by making exercise a habit. It keeps stress levels balanced as too much mental pressure can damage overall health, leading to severe illnesses.

Release of Endorphins

When you engage your body in healthy workouts and exercise, you enable the release of feel-good chemicals known as *endorphins*, which help in enhancing your well-being. Consider non-competitive aerobic exercise, strengthening with weights, or movement activities like yoga or Tai Chi, and set reasonable goals for yourself. Aerobic exercise, like swimming, walking, and rowing, has been shown to release endorphins—natural substances that help you feel better and maintain a positive attitude.

Release of Proteins

You don't need to engage in high-intensity exercise to reap its overall health benefits. By doing a low-intensity activity, you can activate the body for the release of proteins known as *neurotrophic* or growth

122

factors. These proteins contribute to our nerve cells' development and create new connections. Therefore, physical activities are encouraged in children for their growth and in old age so that such individuals can preserve and maintain their health.

Develop a Better Personality

Those who find it challenging to develop self-confidence can build courage with the help of physical activities. This benefit of exercise toward personality growth may surprise many people, but exercise is proven to aid in developing self-confidence and self-esteem.

Physical activity boosts self-esteem by helping you achieve goals that hinder you from facing the public, such as increased weight, poor posture, etc.

When you achieve your desired body weight, you feel more confident to go out in public and meet more people—it even lessens your fears of being bullied for your physical appearance. Also, a confident posture helps ease mingling in social circles and helps you feel better in the workplace while presenting and doing

123

other tasks. Hence, the contribution of physical activity toward personality grooming can help an individual perform better and solidify relationships.

Develop Better Cognitive Abilities

Research proves that people who exercise regularly have a sharper memory than people who do not engage in physical activities. With consistent workouts, our body starts sweating and produces more brain cells that help build memory power. Thus, regular exercise can improve our thinking skills.

For sustainable health of brain cells, exercising provides numerous benefits such as stimulation and release of growth factors, reducing insulin resistance and inflammation, and balancing your sleep cycle.

Sleep Quality

Knowing how sleep can affect our performance and our body's ability to recover from illness is crucial. An imbalance in sleep affects mental health and even impacts cognitive health. Sleep significantly impacts our memory, energy levels, and mood.

With the help of physical activity, we can cure our substandard sleep patterns, which ultimately contribute to our mental and emotional health. Nowadays, we are pressured to meet work standards, deadlines, etc. Unintentionally under pressure, we do not meet the normal level of sleep essential for our well-being. Most people today are suffering from lack of sleep which can become a disorder in the form of insomnia.

Surprisingly, people with severe insomnia who can hardly sleep for two hours per day start overcoming their sleeping problems with the help of regular exercise. It helps regain the lost balance of many areas of our brain and body, thus easing the issues we struggle with daily.

Aerobic Exercises

Stress researchers have found aerobic exercises quite effective for lowering the anxiety levels of many individuals. Consistent findings prove that people who engage in aerobic exercise start feeling calmer about twenty to thirty minutes later. The good thing about practicing aerobics is that the calming effect lasts for several hours.

Soothing stretches help reduce stress by addressing a variety of psychological problems. Stretching improves blood circulation and relaxes our muscles which become stiff and tense during phases of depression. It also decreases joint stiffness, relieving pain and tension in many parts of the body.

It is also surprising to know that the built-up toxins in our body can be drained and released by the simple method of adopting soothing stretches. Moreover, stretching encourages the release of endorphins, which help reduce pain, elevate mood, and provide a sense of tranquility.

If you are not comfortable practicing workouts, stretching can be the most convenient method to derive maximum benefits from doing physical activity.

Yoga

Yoga is a powerful tool to provide strength, harmony, and awareness in the mind and body. The power of yoga lies in the belief in our body's natural tendency toward health and self-healing.

Yoga is a movement-based stress relief technique that provides parasympathetic benefits. It contributes to the efficient functioning of our nervous system by managing the release of stress hormones such as cortisol. It also enables the release of the happiness hormone serotonin, which regulates our emotional balance and ensures long-term contentment.

This exercise method is a good initiative for busy people who intend to calm their negative self-talk. Yoga is an effective way to quiet one's mind and body, build stamina, and build a more assertive personality.

Yoga provides innumerable benefits, including alleviating asthma, bad eyesight, and issues with menstruation, pregnancy, memory, back pain, heart problems, obesity, arthritis, and diabetes, among others.

The harmful effects of stress can be cured by yoga. Unknowingly we experience severe stress levels that later manifest in insomnia, back pain, neck pain, unexplained headaches, drug addiction, and loss of concentration.

Yoga can reduce the harmful effects of stress that affect our physiological health, such as muscle and joint pain. For instance, we can eliminate chronic pain by using dynamic or yin yoga, which releases our mental pressure and cures our stress. Yin yoga is a meditative practice that offers a chance to turn inward and nurture the calm, quiet center that is innate in all of us. It is a practice in stillness, patience, and non-reactivity.

Yin Yoga has multiple benefits to not only the body, but the mind as well. For example, the yin practice can help the body restore range of motion by lengthening the muscles and organs, tendons, ligaments, which by holding a pose, can leave you feeling as though you've had a massage. Because the yin poses force us to slow down, Yin Yoga offers a chance to engage in mindfulness and self-compassion by observing, nurturing, soothing, and calming ourselves. Furthermore, Yin Yoga can tap into the parasympathetic nervous system by using diaphragmatic breathing or belly breathing, which can benefit issues with tension, blood pressure, sleep, digestion, immune function, and stress.

Yoga can also cure mental disturbances such as lack of sleep by releasing hormones that balance our sleep cycle. It also contributes to the development of coping skills and a more positive outlook on life.

Apart from alleviating hundreds of psychological problems, one of the best benefits we can derive from yoga is the management of our stress levels. As stress levels are known to have devastating effects on the mind and body, the powerful tool of yoga alleviates such problems by helping us get in tune with our mind, body, and inner self in safe and calming ways.

Deep Breathing

Deep breathing is crucial in improving a person's physical and mental well-being. Practicing yoga regularly with the proper manner of breathing patterns can provide a variety of benefits, some of which are as follows:

- Creates mental clarity
- Helps increase awareness
- Relieves our chronic stress patterns
- Contributes to mind relaxation
- Helps in muscle relaxation
- Sharpens concentration and attention
- Lowers the risk of pulmonary diseases

Spend Time Outdoors

Spending time close to nature is considered the ultimate de-stressor. Research shows that spending time in a natural setting for even ten minutes can make an individual feel happier and lessen physiological and mental stress.

Ideally, about ten to fifty minutes in natural spaces, including exposure to sunlight and fresh air, is one of the most effective ways to improve our physiological markers such as heart rate and blood pressure. It also increases our focus, stabilizes our mood, and gives us relief from mental strain.

Many therapists today recommend spending time in

nature as a remedy to ease depression and anxiety while strengthening physical and mental health.

Stress Balls

Stress balls are one of the convenient tangible options for improving focus and attention and relaxing our minds during intense, stressful situations. Stress balls are widely used to deal with many issues related to a person's mind and body. It is a handy tool we can use to overcome our everyday stressors.

Stress balls are primarily intended to relieve anxiety and tension. These stress-relief tools contribute to many physiological benefits for individuals. As mind and body are integrated, a cure in the body provides relief to the mind and ultimately helps a person overcome stress and feel more alive. Some contributions of stress balls toward an individual's overall health are as follows:

- A cure for arthritis pains
- Attainment of emotional stability
- A balance in mood swings

- Lower depression and anxiety
- Improved concentration
- Enhanced creativity
- Motivation and a positive mind
- Strengthened muscle and tissues
- Improved sleep

When a stress ball is squeezed, our nerves and muscles stimulate and contract. This stimulation and contraction make them stronger. The strength we achieve by moving our body using the stress balls creates an internal balance in our bodies. Our stress levels are reduced as the stress hormones become balanced, and our overall nervous system is improved by doing specific exercises with the stress balls.

A Short Message from the Author

Hi, are you enjoying the book thus far? I'd love to hear your thoughts! Many readers do not know how hard reviews are to come by, and how much they help an author.

I would be incredibly thankful if you could take just 60 seconds to write a brief review, even if it's just a few sentences!

Thank you for taking the time to share your thoughts!

CHAPTER 7: CONNECT WITH OTHERS

"A good way to overcome stress is to help others out of theirs." —**Dada J. P. Vaswani**

Finding a support system to connect with others is considered an essential factor in minimizing the effects of stress on mental and physiological health. The benefits we derive from positive social support are long-term and aid in sustaining our well-being.

Good social support would mean seeking out those who can:

- Be available in times of need
- Make others feel welcomed and accepted
- Help others through challenging situations
- Assist others in regaining their self-esteem and confidence in life

Types of Social Support

We can find support from people in many forms. Following are the types of social supports that benefit an individual according to their unique nature and situation:

Tangible Social Support

This type of social support includes sharing material or financial resources. If possible, provide financial assistance to your relations, subordinates, or companions.

Connecting with others by providing monetary assistance can ease their stress and bring a feeling of contentment as a reward for your good deed. Tangible aid can include the repayment of loans, paying a child's

136

fee, helping a friend move to a new place, etc. Even arranging meals for those who cannot afford them will help you build strong bonds with other people. Such acts of kindness will also help you gain the trust of many and build a strong image in society. Initiating and maintaining good relationships is vital for leading a happy life.

Informational Support System

As the name indicates, this type of connection with people involves sharing valuable pieces of information with someone who is presently dealing with a stressful situation. By sharing your personal experiences and conveying how you dealt with a stressor, you can ease the other person's stress and anxiety.

Sharing one's struggles can help significantly lessen the other person's mental pressure as they feel they are not alone, and a sense of belonging is regained with the help of this helping gesture. You can also be a valuable member of your support group by directing a depressed person toward the right medical practitioner.

Emotional Social Support

A network comprising emotional social support will care for your feelings and emotions. It includes affirming one's worth, sharing positive regard, and reverence toward one another. Receiving concern and care regarding one's feelings is also one benefit of connecting with people who value your sentiments. Such relationships assure that other people are valued and being listened to. Moreover, people realize that they can rely on another person in times of need, and they have a shoulder to cry on in phases of deep sadness.

Belonging Social Support

This connection with people enables an individual to feel a sense of belonging and have exposure to social leisure. It benefits both the person who decides to join such positive circles and those already part of the group, as they begin to share their mutual happiness.

Spending time with people who feel alone and depressed will help elevate their stress levels and create a feeling of inner peace for you.

138

Why Is It Crucial to Have a Good Social Support Network?

Research provides evidence regarding several mental and physiological health benefits of connecting with people. Positive social support contributes to a person's well-being in surprising ways.

There are many reasons why connecting with other people is essential and valuable for personal growth and maintaining a healthy balance. Some of the benefits that we derive by connecting with others and developing strong social ties are as follows:

- Better immune and endocrine function
- A positive adjustment to chronic disease
- Effective buffering against the harmful effects of stress
- An overall decrease in anxiety levels and depression
- Enhancing self-esteem and building a confident personality
- Promoting a healthy way of living
- Lowering cardiovascular risk

- Increased motivation and creativity
- Helps develop the ability to cope with everyday stressors

Build Healthy Relationships

The benefits we can derive from connecting with the right people are numerous. By adopting this habit, we can mold our lifestyle to keep us happy and stress-free for more extended periods. We can improve our lives and those around us by maintaining a good social support network. Some of the ways to develop good connections with people are as follows:

Make Someone Happy—Lift Others Up

Connecting with people is not solely to loosen oneself and relieve the build-up of stress. It also means becoming a source of strength and motivation for other people. You can make people realize their worth by learning that they are not alone.

It is never too late to cultivate important relationships. A strong connection with people will help you cope
140

with the stress of tough times. You will feel the unmistakable joy of sharing happiness by doing something for others. Try to add excitement to someone's life by throwing a surprise party at your workplace or on weekends. Add a smile to someone's life today and let them know how grateful you are to have them around you.

Listen To Others

Become a volunteer to help others. Sometimes counseling, advice, or suggestions do not allow other people to cope with stressful situations. If you show your availability as a good listener, the stressed-out person will feel they can share their problems and the things that are becoming the cause of anxiety for them. By listening to the issues, you lessen the difficulties and burden of the other person.

Join a Social Group

Connecting with the right type of people is crucial to lowering stress levels. You can join classes or sessions in the field related to your passion or a specific group such as a religious, service, hobby, recreational, civic, or exercise group. For instance, if you join a yoga class to build your physical strength and stamina, you can use this passion to connect with other yogis to develop good friendships and work collectively on your mental and physical improvement.

Overcome Social Isolation and Loneliness by Socializing with People

The state of loneliness exposes a person to various physiological problems such as poor cardiovascular and mental health and the inability to develop and improve one's personality.

It is vital to meet with people who share similar interests and values with you. Also, being available to those who require guidance and help will make you a better person and prove beneficial for the other person in gaining back lost confidence.

Share Your Knowledge and Gifts

Your act of kindness doesn't need to include helping someone through money or by lending only tangible things. You can become a source of happiness for others by doing charity or volunteering your services.

142

For instance, helping someone clear their debts is one way you can lessen the other person's financial and mental burden.

A simple act of helping someone with their unfinished tasks is an excellent way to build a strong foundation of trust and belief. You can also extend a friendly gesture by sending flowers to your loved ones you cannot meet due to work or distance. Maintaining happy relationships with friends and acquaintances is vital for a person to stay motivated and achieve healthy progress in life.

If you possess an ability that can add some joy to the life of a stressed person, do not hesitate to share your gift with them. If you have baking talent, you can surprise someone by visiting with a cake. You can even initiate a friendship with your neighbors by helping them learn the art of baking. You can quickly spread happiness and maintain healthy relationships by sharing your delights with others.

Spend Time with Like-minded People

Spending time with like-minded people can positively impact your cognitive health and ultimately aid in reducing your stress levels. When you lack social support, you may begin to prefer isolation, leading to consistent negative thought patterns.

If you have a tiresome day at work or are going through a financial loss or general confusion, you can reach out to a trustworthy comrade or a family member to share your heart and lessen your mental burden. For instance, a quick chat with a neighbor or a coffee break with a good colleague with whom you can share your worries is an excellent way to lessen your stress levels.

Keep a Balance in Relationships

It's essential to maintain a healthy balance between relationships with family and friends. One should be careful not to overwhelm others with phone calls and unnecessary emails. While building good ties with someone, respecting the other person's time and schedule is mandatory.

Know When to Seek Professional Help

Stress is a typical reaction to everyday pressures and stressors. It becomes mandatory to seek professional treatment in cases where self-help and stress management techniques no longer work to treat our prolonged stress.

Untreated high-stress levels can seriously impact our lives by disturbing our routine, making us feel exhausted, and slowing down our pace and quality of life. Expert advice is necessary when stress takes a more severe toll on our mental and physical health.

The following symptoms, if experienced for more extended periods, might be an indication that you require medical help:

Mental and Emotional Effects

- Feeling distracted
- Fear, nervousness, or anxiety
- Too much worrying
- Being overwhelmed by your expectations

- Disturbed sleep—either sleeping too much or too little
- Inability to make a decision
- Experiencing difficulty sticking to a conclusion

Physiological Effects of Stress

- Persistent tiredness or fatigue
- Headaches and laziness
- Nausea and vomiting
- Chest pain
- Fast heartbeat
- Choking
- Shortness of breath

Following are a few questions or considerations that will help you know if you can cope with your stress by non-pharmaceutical methods or if you require a checkup from a physician or a psychologist.

1. Do you find socializing challenging and feeling irritable around other people?

2. Have you experienced abnormal changes in your eating habits?

3. Do you find it challenging to make a decision or stick to your final decision?

4. Do you depend on alcohol or relaxants to manage your stress?

5. Do you take any unprescribed medicine?

6. Do you often feel lethargic or lack energy?

7. Do you have difficulty sleeping?

8. Do you lose control of your temper in minor situations?

9. Are you prone to mild aches, allergies, coughs, or colds?

10. Do you have gastrointestinal problems such as diarrhea, constipation, or an upset stomach?

11. Have you observed loss or gain of your body weight?

12. Is your sleeping time different from the required sleep time (8 hours)?

Support Groups

Support groups may be offered by a nonprofit advocacy organization, clinic, hospital, or community organization. Formats of support groups vary, including face-to-face meetings, teleconferences, or online communities.

Support groups are not the same as group therapy sessions. Group therapy is a specific type of mental health treatment that brings together several people with similar conditions under the guidance of a licensed mental health care provider.

Benefits of support groups

The shared experience among support group members often means they have similar feelings, worries, everyday problems, treatment decisions, or side effects. Participating in a group allows you to be with

148

people who are likely to have a common purpose and understand one another.

Benefits of participating in a support group may include:

- Feeling less lonely, isolated, or judged
- Reducing distress, depression, anxiety, or fatigue
- Talking openly and honestly about your feelings
- Improving skills to cope with challenges
- Staying motivated to manage chronic conditions or stick to treatment plans
- Gaining a sense of empowerment, control, or hope
- Improving understanding of a disease and your own experience with it
- Getting practical feedback about treatment options
- Learning about health, economic, or social resources

When you join a new support group, you may be nervous about sharing personal issues with people you don't know. At first, you may benefit from simply listening. Over time, however, contributing your ideas and experiences may help you get more out of a support group.

Try a support group for a few weeks. If it doesn't feel like a good fit, consider a different support group or a different support group format.

Remember that a support group isn't a substitute for regular medical care. Let your doctor know that you're participating in a support group. If you don't think a support group is appropriate for you but need help coping with your condition or situation, talk to your doctor about counseling or other types of therapy.

Medical Treatment

Suppose self-management of stress does not produce the desired results for you. In that case, it is best to ask your doctor to refer you to a recommended mental health professional who specializes in treating prolonged anxiety and stress.

You do not need to stay frozen or sit idle waiting for your untreated stress to diminish on its own. Sometimes, negligence can result in serious health issues.

If you feel overpowered by stress, ask for help from a health professional. Certified counselors, medical therapists, psychologists, and psychiatrists are the experts in the mental health field. They can find better treatments and medications to help you cope and reduce your stress and also enable you to become more functional in your day-to-day activities.

You should seek help right away if you have suicidal thoughts, are overwhelmed, feel you cannot cope, or are using drugs or alcohol more frequently as a result of stress. Your doctor may be able to provide a recommendation, or you can find resources to help you find a mental health provider by visiting www.nimh.nih.gov/findhelp.

CHAPTER 8: MAKE TIME FOR FUN AND RELAXATION

Manage Your Time, Don't Let It Manage You

Stress management is often related to better ways of managing one's time. Today, many people are concerned about not using their time well as they feel they do not have enough time to meet their everyday goals or deadlines at work. Learning to manage time effectively and reduce daily stress through proper guidance is possible.

Time Management Tips

Many situations are uncontrollable and can trigger anxiety. Learning better stress and time management principles is crucial before we become helpless in our tight schedules. The following are some tips and strategies that can help us achieve reasonable control over our plans and hours without over-stressing ourselves:

Don't Be Too Strict on Yourself

Practice self-motivation. Appreciate that you've tried and worked hard to achieve your set goals. Our efforts carry importance, as much as a perfect technique for doing a task would matter. Keeping a positive effort toward time management will help you keep things in control.

Create a To-Do List Each Day

It is helpful to plan your goals every day. You can save what you intend to do daily in your cell phone's notes or on a sticky note you use in your dressing room, whichever seems most convenient to you. The primary purpose of time management is to create a feeling of confidence and contentment that things are in balance

154

and that you are putting your efforts into achieving the desired progress in life. Adopting the practice of planning daily goals will make you feel less anxious and more motivated at the same time.

Seek Assistance if Necessary

Recognize signs of being overwhelmed by situations. If you have a time management problem and are overstressed, reach out to someone you trust to help lessen your burden. Sometimes when we have several tasks far greater than the time available, accepting help from a trustworthy person can help us complete the job and relieve stress. If you can assign duties or share responsibilities with others, list everything you need to complete and delegate specific tasks to others.

Be Certain of Your Priorities

Sometimes, we question our abilities to do something and misinterpret situations as stressors. When self-doubt dominates, you falsely believe doing more will make you happier. Try to figure out whether it's the quality or the quantity of time that is important to you. Sorting out things according to their importance will help you take hold of your time and reduce your stress levels. It may be tempting to multitask to accomplish more, but focusing on one task at a time is often better. This strategy can ensure your full attention is on that task so you can efficiently complete it before moving on to the next item.

Be Realistic

No matter how well you prioritize, there is only so much you can achieve in one day, and some distractions are impossible to avoid. It's essential to be realistic when setting goals and prioritizing. Otherwise, you'll create false expectations of those around you and constantly feel like you're falling behind.

Take One Day at a Time

It is never too late to make positive changes in your life. You might feel like spending an excessive amount of time doing things that are not important, such as spending too much time on social media. These activities do not reflect your values and priorities and can even interfere with your normal sleep patterns and other habits vital for your health.

Take one day at a time to safely alter your bad habits into productive ones. Sync your time according to what matters in life, such as family, health, and career.

Observe how much time you spend scrolling and on other unnecessary habits. Gradually cut your time spent on these things from hours to minutes every day. This practice will help you take control over your daily routine, and at the same time, you will feel less irritated as you slowly leave your addictions behind.

Don't Become a Victim of the Time Management Trap

Many people face difficulty in time management due to poor organizing skills, self-doubt, or confusion. Time cannot actually be managed, only our response to a task. All we can do is manage the task/ tasks that we have and how long we have to do them. It is a commonly observed time management trap that people claim they do not know how time rushes by so fast before they can utilize it for productive purposes. In other cases, the actual time available is misinterpreted. People either underestimate the time each task or project will require or overestimate the amount of time they have available. These perceptions make a person either too lazy to finish the work on time or too committed to rush through the task in the short window of time that they do have. It is vital to map out your schedule and every day responsibilities to master time management.

Do Not Exhaust Yourself Over Finances

As trends keep changing and the competition in almost every field is accelerated, it is becoming increasingly common for individuals to work more than their personal capacity and physical stamina. People exhaust themselves with work because their finances demand so, by working overtime or even working more than one job. Planning one's expenditures carefully is also a part of time management, as it takes the majority of your day to make money. You can take control of your expenses by planning to spend less on certain commodities, save more money, pay off utilities, and earn sufficiently by making sure to get paid what you're worth.

Keep Your Surroundings Tidy

Organizing one's environment is as vital as managing

158

one's daily schedule. People often cannot realize the time consumed and wasted in a chaotic environment where things are difficult to find, and achieving a state of mental relaxation can be a challenge. Whether at work or home, staying organized can stop you from draining your time and energy over the messy surroundings and help you better focus on your goals.

Know Your Limits and Boundaries

Be certain regarding your capacity to take responsibility. You should be careful not to take on new activities unless you find a way to pencil them in if your schedule is too tight and completing tasks is difficult for you at the end of each day. By knowing your limitations, you can avoid becoming overwhelmed, stay calm, and adjust to the available time.

If you keep experimenting with your health by putting yourself in a position of taking on more than you can manage, you could develop serious illnesses. Maintaining a balance between your capacity and tasks helps with better time management and improves your quality of life.

159

Set Aside "Me Time"

You know that time to yourself is vital to your health –
but are you getting enough??

"Me time" is time you set aside to be present with
yourself. Taking time to care for yourself is vital to
maintaining health, happiness, and productivity. "Me
time" doesn't have to be a whole day at the spa. Just a
few minutes squeezed into the middle of the day works
if that's all you have. You should find a little time every
day to relax and recharge, so whether it's 20 minutes
or a couple of hours, find ideas and activities to help
you make the most of the time you have all to yourself.

"Me time" can be spent in a variety of ways; what may
feel like "me time" to one person may not feel like "me
time" to another. For one person, it might be spent in
solitude, alone with one's thoughts and engaging in
mindfulness activities. For another, it might be spent
in the community with friends and loved ones
pursuing a hobby.

We often wish to do something we enjoy but then give
up because we don't have enough time for it. Most

160

individuals spend too much time taking up tasks that we *must* do and neglect what we *like* to do. Not having time for self-care and the things that interest you can leave you feeling unhappy and depressed. To shed this unhappiness, adopt the healthy practice of setting aside "me time" for personal contentment and relaxation.

Music Therapy

Sometimes, belting out the lyrics to a favorite tune, no matter the song, makes everything seem all right. If you're in a public place, just listening to music can quickly fix a bad mood.

Music can be a therapeutic tool to reduce stress and promote overall health and healing. The use of music as a stress management technique provides therapeutic benefits to individuals suffering from prolonged depression and anxiety. Music can be incorporated into your routine to fight stress by playing a musical instrument, listening to your favorite type of music, singing along to music, using guided imagery with music, or dancing to your favorite music beats. Classical music can be incredibly relaxing right before bedtime.

Music can trigger the production of dopamine, the "feel-good" hormone. Therefore, a person exposed to music therapy feels happiness, pleasure, and mental relaxation. Music is usually considered a spontaneous activity, though we can use it as an intentional strategy to improve our health.

Musical therapy is a way to treat mental and physical imbalances for many people. It is one of the most economical methods of treating feelings of depression and anxiety. Therefore, it can influence physiological and psychological processes and is widely used to lessen pressure on individuals. Music therapy provides overall relaxation by decreasing the heart rate, balancing temperature, and muscle activity when music is used in the relaxation process for stress relief. Music can provide a non-threatening exciting experience for most individuals and works best for a stress reduction treatment.

Find New Hobbies

Do you remember doing something that used to make you feel great and happy, but now you don't feel like you have enough time to enjoy the things you love? No matter how busy your life gets with changing trends and new daily challenges, you can still spare at least thirty minutes to fulfill your heart's desires. The things you used to find solace in can be incorporated again into your busy routine by just sparing and setting aside a piece of time every day for self-care and self-love. The hobbies which you may like can include reading, playing cards, using acrylic paints, baking, etc.

It is not just refreshing your old hobbies that will improve your life—you can take the initiative to start a fascinating new hobby to change up your monotonous schedule and feel lighter and happier.

You can even take on challenging tasks as new hobbies so that your relaxation time can also prove valuable for you. It could include activities that will not exhaust you physically or mentally but will improve your skills in a particular field or subject.

163

For instance, you may have an interest in being a writer or an author. You can pursue a fresh start in this field by publishing articles on health, awareness, human rights, and humor.

Hobbies are always fun and healthy regardless of a person's age. You can add or alter your habits in any phase of life whenever you realize the importance of change for your stress relief.

The Power of Laughter

We might think of the famous quotation, "laughter is the best medicine," as merely a simple statement. Still, laughter can truly provide surprising benefits that will contribute to your well-being in many ways.

Whether we laugh at a sitcom, a hilarious viral video clip on social media, or guffawing at a billboard cartoon, we are lessening our depression and minimizing our stress levels. Laughter can reduce your risk of catching serious illnesses. The benefits we derive from laughter include both short- and long-term advantages—laughter should be included as the easiest way to erase sadness and anxiety from one's
164

life.

Short-term Benefits

A burst of good laughter can have many short-term benefits for you. When you laugh, it not only aids in lessening your mental burden, but it can also help in bringing out specific physiological changes such as the following:

- Stimulation of Organs

When a person laughs, they stimulate the intake of oxygen-rich air, improve heart functioning, enhance the work of lungs and muscles, and activate the release of essential hormones by the brain.

- Activates and Balances One's Stress Response

A good laughter session can activate your stress response and ultimately lower your stress level. It can increase and then decrease your heart rate and blood pressure. The feeling that we derive from this series of excitement and calmness induces a state of post-relaxation.

- Soothes Anxiety and Accumulated Tension

Laughter can stimulate blood circulation and regulation. It can relieve muscle tension and aid in the relaxation of stiffed muscles. Thus, laughter can reduce the physical symptoms of stress by providing comfort and muscular rest to our bodies.

Long-term Benefits

Laughter can be beneficial for you in terms of providing long-term benefits. Some of the benefits we receive from laughter are as follows:

- Relieves Bodily Pain

Laughter instructs the body to produce its natural pain killer in times of accident or sudden injury. Thus, by providing a natural method of healing, the simple act of laughter can help individuals ease pain or cope with a painful situation in a less strenuous manner.

- Increases Personal Gratitude

Laughter helps you realize your worth and the worth of those around you. You begin feeling the importance of even minor things that add value to your life and start developing an overall affectionate nature. Laughter makes it easier to cope with difficult situations even if you have to manage everything alone. Just smiling and taking things lightly can help you fight a stressor with less jeopardy and reach the solution more quickly. Laughter increases satisfaction and helps you connect with people in more productive ways that prove beneficial to your entire social circle.

- Improves Mood

Laughter can help reduce depression and anxiety related to bad experiences, past events, or chronic illnesses. Laughter raises one's self-esteem and balances a person's mood swings in times of great stress.

- Improves the Immune System

Negative thinking patterns manifest into chemical reactions that can harm your body by fueling your system with more stress and decreasing your immunity. On the contrary, a positive act of laughter can release hormones that help fight stress and prevent immune-related illnesses.

CHAPTER 9: MAINTAIN BALANCE WITH A HEALTHY LIFESTYLE

"Don't underestimate the value of doing nothing, of just going along, listening to all the things you can't hear, and not bothering." —**Anonymous**

Carving out time for self-care can be challenging—most of us live hectic lives. However, becoming more selfish to focus on one's growth and self-care or finding time for personal development should not be considered a negative trait.

For our mental health and well-being, we must work on ourselves as we strive hard to complete our goals.

169

Empowering oneself to achieve a healthy balance in life should be considered a form of preventive care. You cannot surrender to environmental and social pressures or negative internal distortions. Losing one's mental health over anything is harmful, and if not taken care of, it can lead to severe problems which will require long-term treatments that shatter one's everyday life. To avoid such situations, self-care and compassion should be part of our daily practice to ensure a healthy mind and body.

Practicing self-care would imply a purposeful engagement in strategies that promote healthy functioning and enhanced well-being. Filling one's tank with care and empowerment is vital for developing resilience toward everyday stressors which are likely to happen.

Permit yourself to be number one on your priority list, and it will equip you for every future challenge and allow you to live life at its best. Caring for yourself will guarantee a sound mind, body, and spirit.

Focus on Self-Care

If you want to increase your happiness and mental satisfaction level, try incorporating self-care into your routine and consider it essential for your development and growth. This is one of the best changes we can make in our life to balance our anxiety levels and allow ourselves to reflect on what we like to do.

By knowing your worth and taking care of your mental and physical health, you invest in the most precious thing essential for a happy life. When you take care of all aspects of yourself, you'll realize that you can operate more effectively and efficiently. When your overall health is sound, you'll be able to maintain good personal and external relations. With self-care, you will be able to progress with greater focus without having the burden of illness, stress, and restlessness.

Adopting a self-care routine can provide numerous benefits for every individual. Some of the benefits of prioritizing self-care are as follows:

- Increased energy

- Improved happiness and mental peace
- Reducing burnout
- Reduced anxiety and depression
- Improved resilience
- Improved socialization
- Building strong relationships
- Prevention of disease
- Better immunity to cope with illness

Take Brain Breaks

We must strive to achieve a state of mental peace and contentment in life. In doing so, we cannot take on multiple problems at one time and expect them to be settled without affecting our mental health. Taking small steps toward eradicating issues will help avoid cognitive load and pressure and lead to long-term results. Taking short breaks periodically to recharge productivity and focus is good for your health.

Your mind requires a break from constant thinking and work. You can attain overall peace and stability by turning off your thoughts from time to time in a busy routine. You can reboot your brain through activities you love and by incorporating powerful techniques that can help save time and let you spend time in your own way for self-care.

The Benefits of Downtime

The advantages of downtime are way more than we expect, and they remain unknown to most individuals. We often ignore the need to give ourselves a break from all hustle and bustle of life. As a result, we develop the habit of negative thinking, persistent aggression, isolation, and feeling ill frequently.

Recognize the importance of having downtime no matter how tight your schedule is. It is always fruitful to take care of one's needs. Nurturing oneself is as important as completing other tasks and duties assigned to us. Remember, sometimes it is difficult to regain what you have lost in terms of health. By adopting self-care practices and knowing your priorities and values, you can be in a better place to handle everyday stressors.

Setting aside time for yourself can help you achieve

173

many positive additions to your life, including the following:

- An increase in creativity levels
- Time to develop and explore one's interests
- Strengthened mental health
- Time to plan for your future and stability
- Mental relaxation and peace
- Learning about your goals and potential for new things
- Improvement of your emotional health and its regulation

Setting aside time for oneself is particularly beneficial to a particular type of personality—introverts. Introverts who may find it difficult to express their thoughts, feelings, and struggles with others will find time alone more helpful in managing their stressors and relaxing their mind after a long busy day.

Mindfulness and Meditation

Numerous studies have shown that meditation is an effective stress-management tool. That's because in training the mind to be more open and less reactive, we're better able to cope when life's stressors start accumulating. Rather than being caught up in our stress, meditation teaches us to become observers of specific mental patterns and, therefore, become less affected by them.

If you're assuming meditating means needing to clear your mind of every worry, every judgment, and every thought, think again. It's not necessarily about silencing the mind because the nature of the mind is to think and analyze. It's normal for our minds to be overactive. So, just because your mind wanders all over the place doesn't mean you're doing it wrong. It actually means you're doing it right! The goal is to create more focus. It's simply about observing and accepting experiences in the present moment, whether that's an intense emotion, bodily sensations, your breath, or fluctuating thoughts.

Five to ten minutes of peace is all it takes to reap the benefits of meditation. Find a comfortable spot in a quiet place, focus on your breath, and feel those anxieties start to disappear.

Evaluate Your Needs

Does your perspective of your control over your life empower you or destroy your motivation? Are the questions you ask yourself inspiring you or holding you down?

When you realize you are neglecting a particular aspect of life, create a plan to change your routine to adjust the beneficial activities. You should carefully note your thought patterns and their effect on your performance.

Setting smart and measurable goals is a vital preventive measure to ensure you do not get overstressed, overwhelmed, and burned out in the hustle and bustle of life. An effective plan should be tailored to your life to prevent physical and mental exhaustion.

Carefully note major and minor activities that you engage in each day. Devise a list of different parts of your routine and what they require from you. Be it work, school, relationships, or family, this plan will be helpful for you to know what areas of your life need more time and attention from you. Also, the unimportant things to be removed from the routine can be quickly sorted out.

Think about activities and hobbies that can help you feel better at the workplace, in your learning center, or in your social group. For instance, spending more time with people you love will help you build healthy social connections, build inner confidence, and also help you shed social anxiety.

Consider situations that are becoming the reason for your stress. After recognizing your stressors, you can find ways to address the stress associated with those events. You can overcome the stress cliff in your life by adopting stress management techniques and coping mechanisms. The self-help method can provide an additional benefit of building a strong personality by developing a sense of independence and learning problem-solving skills without relying on others.

Chapter 10: My Challenge to You

"Yesterday is gone. Tomorrow has not yet come. We have only today. Let us begin."
—Mother Teresa

Stress in the form of positive or negative challenges is part of our daily lives. How we respond to the stressors or the methods we adopt to cope with stressful situations will shape our lifestyle toward betterment and a long-term satisfied mind.

There is proven evidence that people experience a

mindful way of living when they adopt stress-releasing practices and achieve great physiological and mental strength. It is my challenge to you to make these sound changes. By adopting the recommendations provided here, you will be able to alleviate your depression and prevail over the stress you find very difficult to manage.

Change Your Mindset, Master Your Emotions

It is vital to attain mental peace to change your perspective regarding how you perceive threats, react to particular stressors, and let your body and mind take the pressure off stressful situations.

By shifting our perspective, we can better hold our emotions directly affecting our mental and physiological health.

As we become the master of our emotions, we can overcome the problems that interfere with our healthy mode of living, such as negative cognitive distortions. When we realize the significance of having a proper mindset, we can let go of built-up anxiety and achieve optimism in almost everything we do. Such a state of mind helps us better identify the meaning and purpose of our lives and better shape our lives according to the desired goals.

Create a Stress-Reducing Lifestyle

There are several ways to relieve stress and live life with its whole essence and meaning. Take a look at how you do certain things that are part of your daily activities, and then consider adopting specific healthy changes to achieve a balanced lifestyle.

Some of the things that you can do differently to manage stress efficiently and move forward in life with grace are as follows:

Learn to Live in the Moment

Living in the present is crucial for a sound mind and body. When we are prisoners of our past, we cannot let go of depression and anxiety. Guilt takes up a significant portion of our thoughts as we feel sad about things we could have done better. Also, having too

181

much curiosity and anticipation concerning the future will make a person stressed and unhappy most of the time. Living in the moment and living every moment to the fullest significantly reduces everyday stress. When we learn to relieve stress in the moment, we can let go of our accumulated negative thoughts and learn ways not to overthink the future.

Maintain a Healthy Diet

Eating healthy and maintaining a balanced diet ensures long-term health and strength and helps to keep stress and depression away.

One can also be sure to have a healthy state of body and mind by consuming certain supplements that will help balance any weakness in the body and aid better cognition and emotional health.

Supplements such as chamomile, curcumin, B-complex St. John's wort, and 5-HTP are proven to benefit an individual's overall health significantly. Also, taking multivitamin supplements can be an excellent choice to strengthen one's mind and body.

Keys Vitamins for Reducing Stress Levels

Specific vitamins play a unique role in reducing stress levels.

Vitamin B12

Vitamin B12 acts as a powerful tool for managing mood. It is known to reduce levels of anxiety and depression and provide numerous other health benefits.

Vitamin D

Vitamin D is used to treat anxiety levels. Studies have proven the effects of vitamin D in reducing anxiety levels in women with type 2 diabetes. Thus, we can conclude that consuming this essential nutrient is crucial to our overall health.

Vitamin C

People report a reduction in their anxiety level when taking vitamin C supplements. It also helps keep a positive mood and contributes to better emotional health.

Additional Stress Management Strategies

Make Stress Your Friend

Often, we experience intense physical sensations when we deal with a stressor. The additional energy our body gives us when going through a stressful situation can be a challenge and can be utilized to respond better.

The movement from a threat response to a challenge-response can become exciting and a way of improvement for a person if the energy boost received under pressure is used to rise above the stressor and not become a victim of mental trauma.

Change the Way You Respond to Workplace Stressors

Daily, we experience hundreds of mini-stressors such as work-related emails, assignments, presentations, and tasks attached to deadlines, which make us feel threatened or overwhelmed and induce anxiety that dominates our minds the entire day.

The workplace can become stressful for us, especially when we perceive every stressor as negative and begin

184

challenging our potential and abilities to manage that stressor.

We may perceive the workload as an intrusion in what we are expected to do or as a hurdle in the way of our set goals. Perhaps this stress at work can be seen as a positive motivational factor in providing us an opportunity to explore our abilities and expand our horizons of success through hard work.

By changing our attitude toward the tasks, we can see them as meaningful and carrying lessons for personal development and growth.

Learn Money Management

You should know the essential tactics to manage your finances wisely. Consider saving and not exercising any monetary transaction that can later become a financial burden in the form of debts, hefty repayments, etc. Make sure you have a trustworthy social support network of people who will be ready to extend a helping hand in times when you need financial assistance.

You can consider safe loans if you want to take the initiative to start a business or expand what you are already doing. Whatever your action may be regarding your work, be careful that your decisions do not disturb your mental peace.

Create a Stress Diary

You already keep a record of your meetings, events, important tasks, etc. Likewise, you can also take note of your emotional health by maintaining a stress diary.

A stress diary can help you identify sources of stress, your response to the stressors, and how you can manage your stress response.

Week One: Monitor & Record Events

The first step toward making any change or strengthening a good trait is recognizing the activities that need to be addressed.

In order to manage stress effectively, you should record the events based on their intensity and the extent to which they trigger your stress response. The

186

mild and severe stressors can be learned by recording how certain events, activities, or other people's behaviors impact our mood and emotional well-being.

Week Two: Review—Identify Stressors, Strengths, Challenges, and Next Steps

Once you learn about the stressful situations that impact your mental and physical well-being, you can identify your strengths to cope with those stressors.

Example:

You can fight back a negative distortion with a positive mantra by saying, "I am stronger than the anxiety I am facing." Such strong and motivational self-talk will help you take the initiative to deal with the stress and strengthen your mind to manage everyday stressors.

You can then sort out ways to improve your lifestyle as you begin to work on your personality and strive to make life better and stress-free.

Week Three: Focus on Creating New Habits

When you have identified your stressors and your abilities to fight those stressful events, the next step is implementing the coping mechanisms in your daily routine. Your focus should be on adopting a new healthy lifestyle that will ensure you a relaxed, contented mind and heart in the long run. By making essential revisions to one's existing habits and creating new habits, you can alleviate stress and anxiety levels to a great extent.

For instance, you can start practicing mindfulness meditation, go for a daily walk with your pet or a good friend, try reading a positive topic before going to bed, and set aside some time for things that actually make you happy every day to keep the stress levels at a balance.

Review and Evaluate Your Stress Levels by Maintaining a Stress Diary

Here's one way that you can start maintaining your stress diary. It will hardly take a few minutes from your busy schedule to write down and keep a check on your mental health. All you need to do is spare a few
188

minutes before you close your day to record the current position of your mental health. By maintaining this stress diary, you can perform a self-evaluation and see how your stress levels drop down with the help of careful monitoring and planning.

Stress Diary Example

WEEK 1

DAY	MY EVENTS	STRESS: LOW	MODERATE	HIGH	RATING (1-10)	THE STRESSOR	MY RESPONSE TO
1.	Workpla ce Stress						
2.	Personal Relation ships						
3.	Social Media						
4.	Meeting Deadlin es						

5.	Dealing with Physical Weakness					
6.	Life Adjustments					
7.	Financial Problems					

Conclusion

Stress should not keep you from living your life to the fullest. It's time to tear down your current way of thinking and rebuild thought patterns that contribute to your life in constructive ways.

We have aimed to provide you with vital instructions and stress management techniques throughout this book to help you deal with everyday anxiety and chronic stress. An insight into the nature of stress is crucial to getting rid of built-up anxiety and depression. This book provides an understanding of the root of the stress response that starts in your nervous system and impacts your overall well-being. You have learned numerous stress management strategies and tips that will help you tackle your stress levels and also aid you in healthily molding your lifestyle.

You will surely draw maximum benefits from the stress-relieving techniques in this book. It will help you cancel your negative distortions and help you welcome life with a positive outlook and attitude. You will surely achieve sound mental and physical health by practicing the guidelines mentioned in this book and learning to live your life to the fullest. Through the techniques listed in this book, we hope you will recognize your symptoms of stress, burnout, or cognitive distortions that have prevented you from moving forward into a happy, healthy, stress-free life.

There will be challenges as you seek recovery; however, there is light at the end of the tunnel. When you put in the effort and allow yourself to have hope, you've already started to shift the mindset that confounds you. As you embark on your journey, you may cry and feel upset, but those feelings are all part of the process because recovery requires you to face some uncomfortable truths. You cannot allow that discomfort to discourage you from persevering.

Thank you for reading!

One more thing

If you enjoyed this book and found it helpful, I'd be very grateful if you'd post a short review on Amazon. Your support does make a difference, and I read all the reviews personally so I can get your feedback and make this book even better. I love hearing from my readers, and I'd really appreciate it if you leave your honest feedback.

Thank you for reading!

Bonus Chapter

I would like to share a sneak peek into another one of my books that I think you will enjoy. The book is titled ***"How to Deal with Stress, Depression, and Anxiety: A Vital Guide on How to Deal with Nerves and Coping with Stress, Pain, OCD, and Trauma."***

Are you tired of wasting your time and energy worrying all the time? Do you see the irrationality of constant worrying, but you can't seem to stop doing it? Are you ready to learn how to deal with anxiety and depression without taking drugs?

This book will walk you through precisely why, how, and what you need to do to stop worrying and start living your life.

Nearly 800 million people worldwide experience

197

mental illness. Some of the most prominent adverse mental conditions include stress, anxiety, and depression. These issues can affect your psychological and physical health, and when you let them go untreated, they can have longstanding effects on your life and relationships. The more you ignore your mental strife, the harder it becomes to be resilient in the face of hardship, and if you let emotions get out of hand, they can lead to increased mental illness.

Though stress is an inseparable part of our lives, we can easily manage it using simple strategies and techniques. All we need is the willingness to learn these techniques and the ability to take action. Effective stress management is critical to your physical, psychological, and emotional health. It's vital to your overall well-being. This book will show you how to start managing your issues and get relief immediately.

How to Deal with Stress, Depression, and

Anxiety provides a complete framework and a well-rounded set of tools to understand the causes of stress, depression, anxiety and how to overcome it.

Enjoy this free chapter!

Virtually all people experience stress, anxiety, or depression at various points in their lives. One 2017 study suggested that about 792 million people worldwide have formal mental health disorders, with depression and anxiety being the most common conditions. Millions, maybe even billions, of additional people experience subclinical conditions and high levels of stress, so the number of people who deal daily with such issues is quite astounding. When you live with any of these conditions, everyday activities become a challenge, and you may resort to self-sabotaging behaviors, or you feel stuck in place.

As these conditions continue, it only makes you feel worse, both mentally and physically. In the United States, it's been reported that stress affects the mental health of 73 percent of the population, leading to worsening conditions like depression and anxiety. While these conditions are all too common, they don't have to be. Living with mental illness or stress can feel impossible, and that's a hard burden to carry, which is why mental distress often leads to further mental and emotional anguish.

The Challenge

With so much external pressure in today's society to be their best selves, millions of people worldwide struggle to maintain their mental health and professional or personal well-being. Many emotionally and physically harmful behaviors—such as overworking and extreme self-sacrifice—are glorified by society. As people are pushed to do their best work and make room for a personal and social life, they can become consumed by anxiety and worries that impede their progress.

The statistics on stress, anxiety, and depression depict a grim picture. As the most prevalent mental health issue in the United States, according to the Anxiety and Depression Association of America, anxiety impacts over 40 million American adults, representing over 18 percent of the population. Globally, nearly 300 million people have anxiety. People who have anxiety tend to have greater stress levels, and 50 percent of those diagnosed with anxiety will also be diagnosed with depression. Depression rates are also startlingly high, with just under seven percent of the population experiencing major depression at any given time and another two percent experiencing persistent depressive disorder, also known as dysthymia or chronic depression.

Even if you don't have a clinically diagnosed issue, such as depression or anxiety, you likely have some degree of stress that makes it harder to function as you'd like to. The Global Organization for Stress says that 75 percent of people are moderately stressed, and nearly all people experience stress at some point in their lives because of a myriad of contributing factors. With so much mental dysfunction, it's no wonder that some people think they'll never get better, but this grim picture doesn't have to be your reality.

While mental health conditions have the power to destroy and debilitate people—paralyzing them and making it hard to have hope for the future—there are proven techniques anyone can use to improve their mental health and allow greater opportunity for personal development. You do not need to let your stress, anxiety, or depression hold you back anymore.

The solution to managing your mental health isn't easy or quick, but it is effective. With effort and careful attention to a multi-faceted plan, you can make dramatic improvements to your damaged mental health and start investing more energy into things that make you the most gratified. There are several steps you must follow for the best results. When you apply these steps, you can have increased mental clarity, emotional freedom, and confidence. Curing your mental health issues will require you to face everything that scares you and to admit uncomfortable truths. Still, you'll be far better off when you seek help than the nearly 25 million Americans who have untreated mental health conditions. You may not need the same level of care as people with more severe conditions, but you do need help because living with any degree of stress, anxiety, or depression is living with more pain than you need to have.

Treating a mental illness can seem intimidating to many people, but there are several effective methods, and there are ways to treat, if not cure, any mental health condition you may have. With so many adults and children not currently being treated for their mental health issues, it's no wonder that mental health statistics remain so prevalent. Still, with increased awareness and the greater availability of mental health resources, the prognosis for those who have mental illness continues to improve. Alongside this, as these issues become more widely acknowledged and discussed, the stigmas attached to them are beginning to dissipate, which removes some of the shame linked to mental illness, which only exacerbates it. Accordingly, by committing bravely to treatment and opening yourself to increased understanding of mental illness, you create resilience against mental illness and become more proactive in the treatment of these debilitating conditions.

For those of you with any of these issues, you cannot delay treatment. Mental dysfunction of any kind makes it harder to feel joy and, in the worst cases, it can deprive you of your ability to function. More than that, your mental health can also impact your physical health. For example, research has shown that stress increases the chance of someone dying from cancer by 32 percent. The Canadian Mental Health Association says that people with poor mental health are more prone to having chronic physical disorders.

A study from Johns Hopkins University found that patients with a family history of heart disease were healthier when they engaged in positive thinking. Among the participants of the study, those who had a positive outlook were 13 percent less likely to experience a cardiac event. Additionally, they found that, generally, people who have better outlooks live longer.

The Solution

Recovery is a process that isn't always linear, but this book will lay out the basic steps to help get you on the right track. The first step in the process is all about education. Before you can do anything else, you must understand the beast you're trying to slaughter and the sword you'll use to slay it. You'll learn how the brain works and how problems with its wiring can lead to mental dysfunction. You'll also learn how you can rewire your cognitive processes to promote increased mental health.

In the second step of the process, you'll continue your educational journey and gain a more in-depth understanding of what anxiety, stress, and depression are and how they impact the way you function. You'll start to understand how to address each of these issues using essential coping tools.

Once you've learned about each condition, you'll be introduced to one of the most powerful psychological tools for improved mental health: Cognitive Behavioral Therapy (CBT). You'll discover what CBT is and how to use it to address your mental ailments.

Once you understand the founding principles of these conditions and the fundamentals of CBT, you'll learn how to manage your circumstances daily by overcoming roadblocks and reviving your sense of self by shifting your perspective as you begin to think in new ways. You'll start to care for both your body and your mind in life-changing ways. All of these steps will lead to mental clarity and mental liberation.

With all this in mind, it's clear that a person's mental health impacts every part of their life, and without addressing your mental dysfunction, you'll never have the peace of mind you crave. Each day you do nothing about your mental health is another day you deprive yourself of health and happiness. Your mental health should be your priority, because you cannot fully function as a member of society if you're prohibited from doing all the things you love the most.

If you feel like you are losing sight of yourself and your desires because of your stress, anxiety, or depression, it's time to make a change. It's okay to be nervous about the adjustments you will need to make to feel healthier, but remember that being uncomfortable and uncertain is vital because they represent change. If you don't change, you'll never feel better than you do now. Maybe you have learned to live with your pain and worry, but it's time to learn to live without those negative coping mechanisms because they stop you from living your life to the fullest.

While the techniques in this book can help you improve your levels of stress, anxiety, and depression, I recommend seeking professional support to help push you towards your goals.

There are tons of books on this subject on the market, so thank you for choosing this one! "How to Deal with Stress, Depression, and Anxiety" will provide a complete framework and a well-rounded set of tools for you to understand the causes of stress, depression, anxiety and how to overcome it. Please enjoy!

How Your Brain Works

Too many people hurt their recovery journey by working against their minds. They think they can force their brains into submission, and when that doesn't work, they feel like failures. When a change you're trying to make doesn't stick, it is usually because it isn't one your brain is used to. As much as you may want that change, your brain will resist it because unfamiliar things feel unsafe to the human brain. The human brain loves patterns, and it uses those patterns to create your internal mental programming and perceptions of reality. When you understand how your brain works, you can use it to your advantage to create new patterns and reframe your mental state.

Your brain is a powerful force, and it can work in remarkable ways. In facing your worries, doubts, and other negative feelings, you need to understand how your brain functions so you can stop fighting your brain and start working with it.

Your Map of Reality

In 1931, scientist and philosopher Alfred Korzybski established an important metaphorical notion with his statement, "The map is not the territory." He believed that individuals don't have absolute knowledge of reality; instead, they have a set of beliefs built up over time that influence how they perceive events and situations. People's beliefs and views (their map) are not reality itself (the territory). In other words, perception is not reality.

Your brain fills gaps in understanding automatically. This means that when you don't know something, you subconsciously make an estimation based on the information you do know. When you experience worry or sadness, this can be caused by a map of reality that reinforces those ideas. That worry or sadness lingers in your mind and can shape future decisions unless you reshape your perception. Your map of reality will always be an interpretation, but it can be an

211

interpretation that helps you rather than hurts you. You can change your map of reality and make it more productive by addressing your thoughts and beliefs and how they impact your behavior.

Thoughts, Core Beliefs, and Behavior

Beliefs are sets of ideas that individuals use to dictate how they'll behave. A belief is something you think is a fact. You feel so strongly about something that you're almost positive it's true, regardless of how well you can prove it. You may have some doubts from time to time, but, overall, you consistently stick to those beliefs. Beliefs are attitudes that you fall back on, because they provide a sense of security, and they make you feel that certain things are constant, which is why something that makes you doubt your beliefs can be so painful. Your beliefs drive your unconscious, habitual behaviors. They become so ingrained in you that they feel natural and inherently true.

When you have trouble managing situations or

coping with feelings, you automatically turn to your beliefs for help without exerting too much brainpower. Your beliefs help you determine morality, and they help you decide whether people or things are bad or good. Your whole perspective uses a compilation of your beliefs to fill in the parts of your reality you can't fully understand.

Beliefs are formed based on past experiences and the stimuli around us. Most people's core beliefs— the most driving beliefs they have—are established when they're young children. As they grow older, children commonly challenge the beliefs they've been taught as they begin to think more critically and independently. Nevertheless, many children reaffirm the beliefs they were taught rather than disproving them. As adults, they can challenge these beliefs and, by managing their beliefs, they can create a healthier view of the world that's a more realistic map of reality.

Beliefs can be incredibly powerful. For example,

imagine parents telling their children that paperclips are dangerous. Telling a child that paperclips are dangerous seems silly. Nevertheless, when those words go unchallenged, the child will internalize the message, and they might try to avoid paperclips, which could impede their ability to do certain tasks. But as they grow older, the child would likely challenge that belief and overcome the fear of paperclips.

Other beliefs may be harder to debunk. For instance, if a mom tells her child that dogs are dangerous, the child may become afraid of dogs. This fear could continue into adulthood, because the child has learned to be terrified of dogs. Even rational arguments that dogs aren't something to be scared of may still make it hard for that child to believe. After all, dogs, unlike paperclips, do have the potential to bark and bite. The child would be so convinced by the belief that it would be hard for them to break from that mindset.

You may have beliefs that stand in your way and feel so foundational to who you are that challenging them makes you uncomfortable. Nevertheless, you need to contemplate your limiting beliefs.

While thoughts and beliefs may seem similar, there are some profound differences between them that you must acknowledge if you want to have a complete understanding of how your thoughts and beliefs can make or break your mental health. Thoughts help to form your beliefs. When you have the same thoughts repeatedly, they become beliefs. You become so used to the thoughts that they become ingrained in your subconscious, and it becomes hard to imagine that those thoughts aren't true. Accordingly, when you think negatively, you tend to have a more pessimistic outlook.

Not all thoughts are beliefs. The thoughts that come and go through your mind without repetition never become beliefs. Beliefs are a product of habitual thinking. This means that while it may be hard to break them, you can break them by overwriting those negative thoughts with positive ones, which is a practice that many therapies and techniques discussed in this book use to reduce stress, anxiety, and depression.

As you've seen with the map of reality, perception shapes our views, and it also shapes the way we think. Your thoughts build your beliefs, and your beliefs, in turn, build your sense of what's real. Some of your beliefs will empower you to seek success and find happiness, while others will make the world seem like a dark and scary place with no hope. Try to identify the parts of your belief system that cause you to have negative responses.

Your thought patterns have tremendous power to change your life. The simple act of interrupting negative thought patterns can help you begin to make changes. These changes don't happen overnight, and deeply entrenched beliefs may even take months or years to debunk completely, but, when you focus on the thought patterns you want to instill, you start to question the "truths" you blindly believed.

There will be some beliefs you'll want to keep, and those are ones you can build upon and use to your advantage throughout this process. There's no need to get rid of any belief that's constructive because such beliefs are the ones that help you grow. However, be honest about the beliefs that are hurting you. Many people try to rationalize certain beliefs that they feel psychologically unready to call into question. Open your mind and contemplate, "Is this belief hurting me in covert and manipulative ways?" If you struggle even to pose that question about a particular belief, that belief may be a harmful one.

The way you think isn't something that's out of

your control. According to the Massachusetts Institute of Technology (MIT), 45 percent of your daily choices are habitual, meaning they're a product of your subconscious thought patterns and beliefs. You choose what stimuli you feed to your subconscious. When worries or hopelessness begin to fill your head, try saying to yourself, "The world is a place full of opportunity and good things." While it won't feel like saying this is doing anything at first, rewriting your internal monologue can be a powerful first step toward growth.

When you understand how thoughts and core beliefs shape your behaviors, it becomes easier to create a path for growth. You learn that you're in charge of your beliefs, and your thoughts can only have as much control over you as you give them. You may feel helpless against your negative thoughts, but learning to overcome these harmful thoughts and release the power they have over you is the only way to become a happier person. The more you try to avoid the things that make you anxious, stressed, or depressed, the more anxious, stressed, and depressed you'll become.

Cognitive Distortions

While your brain does its best to give you helpful information and create an accurate perception of reality, sometimes it gets a little lost trying to translate what it observes into a sensible perception. Your brain loves to make connections, and sometimes, it will make connections that are overly simplified and don't show the nuance in a situation. This is called a cognitive distortion.

Simple speaking, cognitive distortions are falsehoods that your brain persuades you into believing are true. Cognitive distortions can take a variety of forms, but one common example is polarized thinking. When you think in polarities, you see things as wrong or right, good or bad, or win or lose. After you fail at one task, you may start to think, "I'll fail every task because I can't do anything right." This perception isn't an accurate one, but you become convinced it's true because your brain has pinpointed what it thinks is a pattern.

The problem with cognitive distortions is that they're often shrouded in negativity. They make you expect the worse, and they convince you that you cannot do certain things or that other things are unsafe. Cognitive distortions change your perspective, and they can quickly become harmful to your overall well-being. If you believe false messages, it's hard to make peace with your situation or feel secure. When you feel insecure, your mental health declines, and your doubts start to make it harder to function normally. Anxiety may take hold, and you may feel more stressed as you try to complete tasks. The hardship of your situation may then lead to depression.

Cognitive distortions can also cause you to act in ways that worsen your mental state. For example, someone with an eating disorder may tell themselves, "Not eating helps me," when they lose a couple of pounds. They keep going with harmful behaviors because a faulty pattern was established of believing that an action is "good," even though the behavior, for obvious reasons, is the opposite of helpful.

Likewise, someone with anxiety may say, "Avoiding this task will make me feel calmer," when procrastination only heaps on the pressure and stress of the situation. Delaying the task may have given them a sense of relief before, so they keep doing it. It continues to impair them, but cognitive distortion causes them to keep repeating the same harmful behavior. Cognitive distortions fool you into thinking certain actions are good for you or that they aren't as harmful as they are. Someone may engage in risky behavior and think, "This won't hurt me because it didn't harm me before," when that's not accurate information. People often use these distortions to justify harmful, habitual behaviors that give temporary relief to mental distress, but this causes more problems in the long run.

Negative Thoughts

Negative thoughts can play an influential role in how your brain works because your thoughts help create your map of reality and form your cognitive distortions. It's much easier to give in to negative thoughts than positive ones. People often expect the worst because they're afraid that having hope will lead to disappointment. Negative thoughts are also fueled by the internalization of negative comments that others have made about you in the past. For instance, if your mother tells you that you're ugly, you may start to think you're unattractive until it ultimately becomes a core belief.

Research has shown how much healthier and happier people are when they think positively because the brain responds to the input we give it.

So, you can change your outlook by thinking with more positivity. When you think negatively, you're feeding your brain with information it can use against you; therefore, give it information that will help you instead!

The Role of Trauma

Trauma is a significant part of human life, and it can be one of the largest contributors to adverse mental health outcomes, including increased depression, anxiety, and stress. According to the National Council for Behavioral Health, 70 percent of adults in the United States have experienced at least one traumatic event, which means that 223.4 million people in the United States alone have had trauma. Moreover, among people who seek treatment for mental health issues, 90 percent have gone through trauma. Consequently, if you have trauma, it contributes to some of the issues you may be experiencing.

Trauma is the result of events that cause deep

worry or distress. Traumatic experiences are often those that either threaten a person's life or the life or well-being of those they love.

You can have both physical and emotional trauma. Physical trauma can be a response to accidents, injuries, or other physical events. Physical trauma often can trigger emotional trauma, and the scars from emotional trauma often linger longer than those of physical trauma. Trauma can result from physical, verbal, emotional, or sexual abuse, and children who live in violent environments are at an increased risk for trauma. Some people don't realize they have trauma. They might say, "Oh, well, what I went through wasn't that bad compared to other people." However, trauma doesn't mean you were tortured or injured in unthinkable ways. The death of people you love or contracting a serious disease can also cause trauma. Anything can be traumatic if it makes you feel unsafe, so don't downplay those feelings—accept how you feel, even if you don't think it's "that bad."

When you have trauma that you haven't addressed, you're bound to have increased mental challenges. Trauma alone doesn't lead to mental illness, but it's a major contributing factor, and it drives you to rely on unhealthy coping mechanisms that do you more harm than good.

Trauma changes the way you think, which can impact your decision-making processes and your unconscious thoughts. Trauma makes your brain feel unsafe, and when your brain feels unsafe, it focuses on protecting you from future pain, because that pain could threaten your survival. Even in circumstances that don't usually cause anxiety, you may start to feel threatened, even if you can't logically explain why. When you go through trauma, your brain has a stress response, and that stress response reacts to the trauma by changing your future behaviors in an attempt to protect you.

The stress response involves areas of the brain, including the prefrontal cortex, hippocampus, and amygdala. These areas experience lingering changes when they undergo the intense pressure of trauma. As a result, the way your brain processes information shifts when you experience trauma. Your amygdala becomes more active. This part of your brain is responsible for your flight-or-fight reactions and, when it's overactive, it can make you feel as though you're in danger in non-dangerous situations. It stays on guard because it wants to prevent any potential threats from sneaking up on you.

When your amygdala becomes more active, you may be more prone to feeling stressed, and the hippocampus—the part of your brain that handles short-term memories—may become less active. As a result, you may struggle to differentiate between things that happened to you in the past and things that are presently happening.

Finally, the pre-cortex may shrink, and when it does, you have trouble dealing with your emotions and regulating your thoughts. Many of these changes can be found in people who have post-traumatic stress disorder (PTSD), but anyone with trauma can experience them to a lesser degree.

For obvious reasons, trauma makes it hard for you to be mentally healthy, but it also makes it hard for you to be physically healthy. When your physical health declines, this creates additional causes of anxiety, stress, and depression. Thus, not only can your mental health make your physical health worse, but your physical health can make your mental health worse. The Canadian Mental Health Association reports that people with depression are three times as likely to have chronic pain than people without depression. People who have chronic pain are two times as likely to have anxiety or a mood disorder. Mental and physical health are often dependent on one another, which is why the correlations between the two are so important.

According to statistics, you are more likely to experience health issues such as chronic obstructive pulmonary disease (COPD), heart disease, high blood pressure, cancer, and diabetes when you have trauma. These conditions can all reduce your life's quality or longevity, which can then create even more mental unrest. That psychological turbulence can lead to your physical conditions worsening. You can see how these situations can quickly become bleak for those experiencing them. However, by addressing your trauma, you can reduce the potency of some of these issues.

Trauma, unfortunately, is a normal part of life. For many people, it's challenging to manage, but it's nothing to be ashamed of. Using the strategies in this book, you can learn to become conscious of your trauma and take away the power it has to control your life. Simple techniques like listening to music, establishing a healthy diet and exercise routine, practicing meditation, and admitting you have trauma are just some of the most basic techniques you can use to recover.

Recovery from trauma is painful, but it's one of the most important things you can do for your health because working through trauma allows you to heal your brain and teach it new patterns.

Get Professional Help

Before you do anything, you should seek professional help. Seeing a doctor or a mental health professional can help ensure that you have a support system in place to help you improve yourself.

While this book's techniques can help you improve your levels of stress, anxiety, and depression, some people will still need professional support to help push them toward their goals. Additionally, for some people, these issues may be related to their brain chemistry, which may require medication. To have a satisfactory recovery experience, you must take a holistic approach that ensures you achieve long-lasting results and can learn coping skills that will shape the rest of your life.

Get your full copy today! *"How to Deal with Stress, Depression, and Anxiety: A Vital Guide on How to Deal with Nerves and Coping with Stress, Pain, OCD, and Trauma."*

BOOKS BY RICHARD BANKS

Assertiveness Training: Learn How to Say No and Stop People-Pleasing by Establishing Healthy Boundaries

The Keys to Being Brilliantly Confident and More Assertive: A Vital Guide to Enhancing Your Communication Skills, Getting Rid of Anxiety, and Building Assertiveness

The Art of Active Listening: How to Listen Effectively in 10 Simple Steps to Improve Relationships and Increase Productivity

How to Deal With Stress, Depression, and Anxiety: A Vital Guide on How to Deal with Nerves and Coping with Stress, Pain, OCD and Trauma

How to Deal with Grief, Loss, and Death: A
Survivor's Guide to Coping with Pain and
Trauma, and Learning to Live Again

Develop a Positive Mindset and Attract the Life
of Your Dreams: Unleash Positive Thinking to
Achieve Unbound Happiness, Health, and
Success

How to Stop Being Negative, Angry, and Mean:
Master Your Mind and Take Control of Your Life

**For the Full Book Listing go to
https://author.to/RichardBanksBooks**